A SOCIOLOGICAL ALMANAC FOR THE UNITED STATES

A SOCIOLOGICAL ALMANAC FOR THE UNITED STATES

SECOND EDITION

EDITED BY
MURRAY GENDELL
AND
HANS L. ZETTERBERG
COLUMBIA UNIVERSITY

New York
CHARLES SCRIBNER'S SONS

Published by arrangement with The Bedminster Press

A-264 [M]

THIS BOOK PUBLISHED SIMULTANEOUSLY IN
THE UNITED STATES OF AMERICA AND IN CANADA

PRINTED IN THE UNITED STATES OF AMERICA

Library of Congress Catalog Card Number 61-14348

ACKNOWLEDGMENTS

Full identification of the material used in this book appears with each table in the text. Unless the place of publication is shown below, it is New York. Grateful acknowledgment is due to the following:

Appleton-Century-Crofts and the Southern Educational Reporting Service, Nashville, Tennessee for Table 8.30, from James G. Cook, *The Segregationists,* copyright © 1962, by Appleton-Century-Crofts

The American Journal of Sociology and Kingsley Davis for Table 9.10, from Vol. 60 (1955), copyright by the University of Chicago

The American Statistical Association and Bernard Lazerwitz for Table 6.30, from the *Journal of the American Statistical Association,* Vol. 56, no. 295 (September 1961)

The American Economic Review and Herman P. Miller for Table 5.60, from "Annual and Life-time Income in Relation to Education: 1939-1959," Vol. 50, no. 5 (December, 1960)

The Bedminster Press for Table 3.51, from Murray Hausknecht, *The Joiners; A Sociological Description of Voluntary Association Membership in the United States,* copyright © 1962 by the Bedminster Press, Totowa, New Jersey

R. R. Bowker, Co. for Table 5.10, based on annual summaries in *Publisher's Weekly,* copyright by R. R. Bowker, Co.

The Brookings Institute for Table 4.42 from Herman M. and Anne R. Somers, *Doctors, Patients and Health Insurance: The Organization and Financing of Medical Care,* copyright 1961 by The Brookings Institute

International Statistical Institute, Kingsley Davis and Hilda Hertz for Table 9.11, from *Bulletin of the International Statistical Institute,* Vol. XXXIII, Part IV, The Hague, Netherlands

Current Sociology and S. M. Miller for Table 4.55 from Vol. 9 (1960)

The City College Press for Table 7.20, from Herman C. Myers, *Problems of the Younger American Artist,* copyright 1957 by the City College Press

Doubleday and Company for the following:

Table 8.10 (in part) from Seymour Martin Lipset, *Political Man,* copyright © 1959 by Seymour Martin Lipset. Reprinted by permission of Doubleday and Company, Inc.

Table 8.10 (in part) from Samuel A. Stauffer, *Communism, Conformity and Civil Rights,* copyright © 1955 by Samuel A. Stauffer. Reprinted by permission of Doubleday and Company, Inc.

The Free Press for the following:

Table 3.40 from Robert Lane, *Political Life,* copyright © 1959 by the Free Press of Glencoe (now New York)

Table 4.10 from Philip M. Hauser (ed.) *Population and World Politics,* copyright © 1958 by the Free Press of Glencoe

Table 6.10 from Michael Argyle, *Religious Behavior,* 1959

Gale Research Company for Table 3.50, from *Encyclopedia of American Associations,* Gale Research Company, Detroit, Michigan

Houghton Mifflin Company for portions of Table 1.62 from Marvin B. Sussman, editor, *Source-*

FROM THE PREFACE TO THE FIRST EDITION

One learns a great deal about society simply by living in it. However, we often need a picture of our society that is not limited by the horizon of any one individual. To have such a comprehensive view is essential not only for the student of society but also for decision makers in law, government, investment, marketing, transportation, welfare, et cetera. The most common way we have to achieve such an over-all view is through statistics. Statistics condenses into one figure, or into a few lines in a table, information about thousands of individuals. Admittedly, statistical summaries and tables do not make particularly easy reading, and few people ever get excited about them. But they do reveal in a quick and precise way what would take numerous man-hours to discover by merely participating in and observing the life around us.

This book features an essay (by Hans L. Zetterberg) giving a statistical summary of the contemporary United States, and a selection of statistical tables (edited by Murray Gendell) presenting some of the sources of the essay in greater detail [as well as additional material not included in the essay].

Most every field has its own special set of statistical tables, and experts watch constantly over the variations that occur in the statistical series. In this book we have not collected tables for specialists in any one field. We want to emphasize gross patterns, and are not overly concerned with the latest fluctuation. By making some comparisons with the past we hope to convey a feeling for long-range trends, and by making some comparisons with other countries we want to give the reader a basis to judge whether the U.S. figure is high or low.

Our collection of tables grew out of a feeling that American college students know too little about their nation. We thought it particularly misplaced that so many sociology students knew more about the terminology and method of sociology than they knew about their society.

PREFACE TO THE SECOND EDITION

This revision updates the statistics, replaces some tables with more adequate ones that now have become available, deletes the least essential tables to make room for something more essential. We have kept the modest scope of the book; we want it to be judged, not by its bulk, but by the discriminating choices made from the huge mass of statistics that is available.

A new numbering system for the tables has been introduced; it is explained in a separate note on the organization of the *Sociological Almanac*. It links our selection of material to criteria of theoretical sociology.

In making these changes we have benefited from much generous advice from teachers who have used the *Almanac* in college classes, librarians who have informed us about the common requests for statistical information they receive, foreign journalists, diplomats and visitors who have pointed out where they want special orientation. A special word of thanks is due to the staff of Charles Scribner's Sons who aided us beyond the call of duty in the final phase of our work.

MURRAY GENDELL HANS L. ZETTERBERG

Contents

Tables

The United States Summed Up by Browsing in A Sociological Almanac

BY HANS L. ZETTERBERG

THE UNITED STATES SUMMED UP
BY BROWSING IN A SOCIOLOGICAL ALMANAC

BY HANS L. ZETTERBERG

Most of us occasionally devote an odd half hour or so to reading facts about our world, our country, or our home town in an annual almanac. The editor of the almanac includes all the information that the public may ask for or find interesting. The scientist has another purpose in mind when it comes to facts and figures; he selects information on all the issues that his science defines as important. From the mass of statistical facts and figures available about the United States, this essay presents a small selection based on a sociologist's conception of what commands special attention (see p. 33). The remarks that follow may serve as strings around the tables in a sociological almanac for the contemporary United States; they intend to tie them together into a manageable bundle, the whole of which can be easily grasped.

1. Human Resources

Persons reaching the retirement age of 65 years in 1964-65 have seen the population of the United States grow from 76 million to 190 million within their lifetime. If they have spent most of their days in the Western states they have experienced an even more rapid multiplication of neighbors, for the population of the West has grown about four times the national average (Table 1.12).

The balance of birth and death, immigration and emigration has been such that the American population showed an increment of about 2 million per year in the 1940's and almost 3 million per year in the 1950's (Table 1.20). This is a remarkably high rate for a modern society, so high that it virtually keeps up with the so-called population explosion in less developed countries. At present, 6 per cent of the world's population lives in the United States. The best projections of future population figures indicate that America north of Mexico will have nearly the same share of world population in 1975 as it had in 1950 (Table 1.10). This is no mean achievement, because the world population grows at an incredible rate; it is estimated that less than 80 billion people have ever lived on this earth and no less than 4 per cent of all human beings of all times live today.

The increase in population has become more and more due to the balance of birth and death, and less and less due to the balance of immigration and emigration. In the first decade of this century, 39 per cent of the population increase resulted from an excess of arriving immigrants over departing ones, while in the fifties only ten per cent of the increase was accounted for by immigrants (Table 1.20).[1] In the eighty years from 1880 to 1960, the proportion of foreign-born in America was decreased from 13.1 to 5.2 per cent (Table 1.40), and a further drop in this proportion can be expected over the next few decades if the present pattern of immigration prevails.

Life expectancy has increased by more than 22 years during this century, and death rates have been cut in half. It is significant that the crude death rate for Negroes, which used to be considerably higher than for whites, is now almost the same as that of whites (Table 1.41). Roughly, one out of every ten Americans is a Negro, and one out of 200 is an Oriental, or belongs to another non-white race. The proportion of non-whites declined from 13 per cent in 1800 to 10 per cent in 1950, but can now be expected to rise again, reflecting their higher birth rates; in 1960, 11.4 per cent were non-white (Table 1.40). Present rates indicate that the non-white population will double in a generation, while the white population will take almost a generation and a half to double.

American women outnumber men by one or two per hundred (Table 1.30), except among the very young and in the West, where there is still a faint echo of the pioneering of men. (However, even in the West the figure has dropped from 15 men per 100 women in 1880 to 102 per 100 in 1950.)[2]

The marriage rate made a remarkable jump right after World War II to an all-time high of 16.2 marriages per 1000 persons, but has since tapered off to rates around 8 marriages a year per 1000 persons (Table 1.63). This rate nevertheless is somewhat above the levels customary in all but a few foreign countries (Table 1.64). The divorce rate has also declined since the war; in 1946 there were 18.2 divorces per 1000 existing marriages; in 1959 there were about half this number, or 9.3 (Table 1.63). Less than half of all divorce decrees involve children (Table 1.65). The divorces do not usually reflect any aversion to marriage as such; for example, over 98 per cent of those divorced before age 30 remarry, most of them within two or three years.[3]

Fewer women in the United States remain single throughout child-bearing age than in any Western country, a fact that goes a long way toward explaining the growth rate of the American population. At the same time, childlessness, which in 1890 was at the level of 8 per cent of all ever-married women past child-bearing age, had risen to 19 per cent by 1952. The figures for the younger age-groups forecast that the present generation of women of child-bearing age has reversed the trend: only one

[1] In the winter 1960-1961, some 1600 Cuban refugees arrived every week in Miami, while in the last few years the total net arrivals from all nations to the United States has been around 5600 a week.

[2] See Warren S. Thompson, *Population Problems*, McGraw-Hill, New York, 1953, p. 92 for regional differences in the United States and some international comparisons.

[3] Paul H. Jacobson, *American Marriage and Divorce*, Holt, Rinehart and Winston, Inc., New York, table 40, p. 85.

out of ten of them is likely to go through married life without a child.[4] Women who were beyond child-bearing age in 1957 had given birth, on the average, to 2.80 children. Catholic women had an averagee of 3.06 children; Protestant, 2.75, and Jewish, 2.22 children. However, one should not generalize about the Protestants: The Baptists had borne more children than the Catholics, and the Presbyterians fewer children than the Jews (Table 1.74). In general, the knowledge of birth control has been used to concentrate births in the years when women are in their (early) twenties. It is extra-ordinary to report that the typical American woman is only 25.8 years of age at the birth of her last child (Table 1.62). Thus the typical American girl is finished with child-bearing about the time the typical girl is Northern Europe gets married.

At the age when young people reach their majority, half of them are already married. One can only speculate why the age of marriage is so low in the United States. Perhaps the combination of strong emphasis on sex in mass-media and strict social norms that frown on pre-marital sexual experimentation puts many teen-agers and young adults in a tense situation of cross-pressure which an early marriage resolves. To this one must add the factor of the nation's prosperity, which enables marrying youngsters to get a good start on a home of their own through financial help from their parents. At any rate, the early marriages, the concentration of the child-bearing period, and the longer life span have brought about other shifts. A comparison of the median age of husband and wife at the turning points of their family cycles in 1890 and 1959 gives a picture of the long-term trends: (1) age at marriage declines from 26.1 to 22.3 for men and 22.0 to 20.2 for women, (2) age at the birth of the last child declines from 36.0 to 27.9 for husbands, and 31.9 to 25.8 for wives, (3) the age of the parents at the wedding of their last child declines by 10 years and takes place when the father is 49.2 and the mother is 47.1, (4) the age to which the couple jointly survives increases, finally (5) the death of the surviving spouse occurs later (Table 1.62). At the same time, the size of the median household declined from 4.5 persons to 3.0 persons (Table 1.71).

In the last few years we have been in a slight decline of marriage and birth rates. The multitude of children born after World War II are now in increasing number reaching their teens. The realization that a teenager costs the parents about twice as much as a younger child is perhaps becoming more vivid in the communities of the nation, and this has a sobering influence on family planning, also among newly formed families.

The children of high school age will double in the 1960's. The age group between 20 and 24 will increase by 90 per cent between 1960 and 1980, while the entire population increases 45 per cent (Table 1.22). Schools, house builders, labor markets, draft boards, et cetera will have to face this, as will parents who, according to the prevailing pattern, sponsor to a large extent, in financial and other ways, the entries of young adults into colleges, jobs, and marriages.

[4] Paul C. Glick, *American Families,* John Wiley and Sons, New York, 1957, p. 66.

2. *Non-Human Resources*

In considering data on the growth of the population of the United States, it is important to remember that size of population alone is not in itself a reliable indication of what a society can or cannot do. Growth may be located primarily in the youngest and the oldest age group, while the productive ages remain more stationary. More important, the potential of a society always includes its use of *non-human sources of energy.* For example, in 1958 the average American used per year 56 times as much non-human energy—from sources such as petroleum, coal, natural gas, and electricity—as the average person in India, and two and a half times as much as the average person in the Soviet Union.[5] (In computing these figures, we have not counted the resources of non-human sources of energy for military destruction, which have recently expanded beyond the limits of the human imagination. At a press conference in the late summer of 1963, President Kennedy indicated that there were enough nuclear weapons available to kill 300 million people in one hour.)

Since in America the production of most goods and services require the use of non-human energy, statistics on the amount consumed constitute one of the better indicators of the state of our economy. The recent developments of electronic data-processing and calculation have led to greater use of non-human sources of energy in the administration of men and in the pursuit of knowledge. The manufacture of these devices represents the fastest-growing American industry since World War II. The social consequences of the use of electronic equipment extend far beyond the displacement of a large, but unknown, number of office workers. The new method of record-keeping and processing enhance an administrator's ability to keep track of his subordinates' actions and hold them accountable for what they have done. The consequence in any private or public government seems to be the opportuntiy for more central planning and less individual privacy and discretion. In science, the new electronic methods of calculation will probably give us better means for prediction of events affected by a large multitude of factors, e.g., health, weather, and social processes. The invention of the high-speed electronic calculator may well do to decision-making and intellectual labor what the invention of the steam engine once did for manual labor.

Exact figures on physical stamina are hard to find and interpret. About five million Americans suffer from permanent disabilities from injuries that happened after they entered the labor force; 3.3 million of them are under sixty-five years of age. On balance, popular active participation in sports is not widespread, except among teenagers (Table 7.2). Tests reported by the American Association for Health, Physical Education and Recreation indicate that American youth is not quite as physically fit as youth in some European countries. A complex societal effect, such as that of the armed services in World War II, could not use more than about

[5] United Nations, *World Energy Supplies 1955-1958,* Statistical Papers, Series J, no. 3, United Nations, New York, 1960, pp. 7, 25, and 35. See also Table 2.00.

half of the eligible men. Some 4.4 million were deferred and 5.7 million men, or a quarter of the men considered for Army service during World War II, were rejected after their induction examination; and an additional 2.5 million were later separated from service, 13 per cent of whom had physical disabilities and 22 per cent psychiatric disabilities (Table 1.51).

The preservation of human resources and physical health ranks high in the American scale of values, as is shown by the large number of health services. The United States had 142 active physicians per 100,000 persons in 1960. This is actually a decline from 155 per 100,000 in 1900. However, the need of the nation for more physicians has been balanced to a considerable extent by new methods of treatment, better sanitation, and more hospitals, and, above all, by the growth of auxiliary health professions. Thus, the number of nurses grew from 55 to 282 per 100,000 population in the period from 1910 to 1960, and nursing is now the third largest profession, outnumbered only by teaching and engineering. For 1960, the American Hospital Association reported 25 million admissions in its 6,876 hospitals, that is, about one admission per seven persons (Table 1.50). The country has over a million and a half hospital beds in virtually continuous use, the largest number being occupied by mentally ill patients.

3. *Polity and Order*

Any governance, whether public or private, is concerned with prescriptions: laws, ordinances, executive orders, decisions, rules, policies, programs, understandings, commands, and traditions are some of the names we give to these prescriptions. Those prescriptions that are consonant with each other add up to what we call the social *order*. The core of a social order is the laws, the codified or traditional prescriptions which are enforced by public government. We do not have any reliable counts of the number of laws, but all observers seem to agree that the number of legally regulated activities is increasing in our society, which is one sign that our social order is growing and becoming more complex.

The public governments in the United States, in addition to the federal one and the 50 state ones, consist of over 102,000 counties, townships and municipalities, school districts, and other territorial bodies.[6] Of particular interest is the emergence, in recent decades, of many so-called "authorities," which combine features of business organizations with features of public agencies. No modern country in the world seems to have decentralized its public government into so many small units as has the United States. Americans have exhibited great reluctance and suspicion toward any great concentration of government authority. Ideology aside, serious questions can be raised about the cost and efficiency of the many small units. Since the end of World War II the amount of federal tax collected has increased 100 per cent but state and local taxes have increased 600 per cent.

Large private organizations have their own "governments" within the

[6] The figure is given in Nathan Miller, "United States", in B. A. Cohen (editor) *The Worldmark Encyclopedia of The Nations,* Harper and Bros., New York, 1960, p, 1075. My own calculations from various sources give a total of about 120,000.

framework set by the laws issued by the public ones. In this category, the U.S. has over a million corporations (Table 4.30) including some 300,000 manufacturing establishments, with an average number of 57 employees.[7] Among the private governments we also include some 250 religious bodies, with about 310,000 local parishes and congregations, averaging about 300 persons in each. Finally, among the important private governments we must also count some 8,700 national voluntary associations (Table 3.50), and the labor unions, to which a third of all employed in in non-agricultural pursuits belong (Table 3.53). America is not entirely a nation of joiners. However, at least 36 per cent of all adult Americans belong to a voluntary association other than churches or unions; memberships are more common among those who own than those who rent their residences—in other words, more common among stable and wealthier persons—more common among the more educated than the less educated, more common among married than single, and less common in big cities than small, but more common in small cities than in rural areas (Table 3.25).

Persons who occupy positions where the production of prescriptions is expected of them are the *rulers* of the social order. They invent new prescriptions, and thus change or enlarge the social order. Those who apply or transmit the prescriptions to others are the *administrators* of the social order, and those who find themselves exposed to the prescriptions are the *subjects*. The present trend is toward a rapidly enlarging body of administrators. Thus the number of persons in government civil service (not all of whom are administrators) increased from 2.6 millions in 1920 to 8.8 millions in 1961. During the last ten years, federal employment grew by 18 per cent, while employment in state and local governments rose 60 per cent (Table 3.20). Those who want to gripe about the growth of government bureaucracy may do well to turn their attention not only to Washington but to their own home town. In industry, the administrators have also increased. Bendix reports 8 administrative employees per 100 production workers in 1899, 18 in 1929, and 22 per 100 in 1947; in 1961 they were 36 per 100.[8] We have no figures on the growth of functionaries in churches, labor unions and voluntary associations.

The maintenance of our social order is, in the last analysis, ensured only by means of the government's use of physical (military or police) force. One should not minimize the extent to which this is exercised as a reality, rather than as a mere threat. In 1961, American cities had 1.9 police department employees per 1,000 population and no less than 3.85 million arrests (Table 3.22 and 3.30). To maintain the external defense of its social order, the United States, in June 1961, maintained 2.5 million men in its military establishment, about a third of whom were based abroad (Table 3.21).

[7] U.S. Bureau of the Census, *Statistical Abstract of the United States: 1963*, Washington, D.C., 1963, p. 773.

[8] *Ibid.* and Reinhard Bendix, *Work and Authority in Industry*, John Wiley and Sons, New York, 1956, p. 214.

Rulers and administrators exercise *power*. We learn which person or organization has power by learning whose version of order prevails. Answers in terms of persons are probably appropriate in some instances—the President of the United States has enormous power—but in many contexts, particularly in highly organized democracies, they appear less appropriate. Here, any power of importance is likely to be not a person but an organization. Organized parties gather up whatever power rests in individual votes. Every branch of the economy has its pressure organization: industrialists, farmers, retailers, laborers, etc., have their lobbies. The religiously oriented use the weight of their organizations, the churches, to impress the body politic. Also, voluntary associations of varoius kinds often exercise considerable power on the local level, where the units of public government are small and weak. "We live in an era in which only organization counts," says Robert S. Lynd; "values and causes with unorganized or only vaguely organized backing were never so impotent."[9]

Power is difficult to measure, and one cannot easily present statistics on the distribution of power in a society. Lawyers, who constitute about one-tenth of one per cent of the population of the United States, supply the majority of its decision-makers in government. For various periods, 70 per cent of all presidents, vice presidents, and cabinet members have been lawyers, and so have 57 per cent of all senators, 56 per cent of all members of the House of Representatives, and 52 per cent of all state governors (Table 3.22). This is not a recent trend, as Matthews points out: "25 of the 52 signers of the Declaration of Independence were lawyers, 31 of the 55 members of the Continental Congress, 23 of the 33 men who have served as President of the United States have been lawyers."[10] These statistics do not necessarily mean that the lawyers have the power; they are for the most part spokesmen for interests other than the bar associations, and advocate the respective versions of order of these interests. Power in the United States is localized in the large organizations of business and industry, in labor and farm groups, and, above all, in the large semi-autonomous branches of government, such as the White House, the Congress, the high courts, and the military establishment.

The task of the government and its various agencies is not only to exercise power by initiating actions but also to maintain orderly market places in which power blocks can fight out their interests and arrive at reasonable and workable compromises. The most important such arenas for decision-making are, of course, the Congress, the state legislatures, and the high courts. They supplement each other. Thus the Supreme Court in the recent decade has made two major decisions that the representative bodies refused to face: racial integration in the schools, and re-drawing of election districts to give voters in urban areas equal weight with voters

[9] Robert S. Lynd, "Foreword" to Robert A. Brady, *Business as a System of Power*, Columbia University Press, New York, 1943, p. xi.

[10] Donald R. Matthews, *The Social Background of Political Decision-Makers*, Random House, New York, 1954, p. 30.

in rural areas in selecting their representatives. It may be noted, however, that decision-making both in Congress and in the courts is becoming dangerously slow. It may be over a year before Congress says yes or no to a request from the President, and it may be several years before a citizen or corporation can get a court decision on a complaint.

Democracy, sociologically speaking, is a protest movement against the uneven distribution of power. Democracy seeks devices to disperse or decentralize power. Ideally, it means that everyone has equal power. In practice, it means that everyone exerts some influnce on the governmental process, by voting for a party in general elections of office holders and by expressing opinions publicly. In 1860 only 17 per cent of the population was eligible to vote; in 1920 adult women got the right to vote; and in 1960 some 109 million Americans, or 61 per cent of the total population, were eligible to participate in the presidential election (Table 3.40). The ineligible are those under 21 years of age, too-recent residents of their states to have voting rights, illiterates, or aliens. Only two-thirds of those who are eligible actually vote; non-voting is greater among women than among men (31 compared to 21 per cent), greater among Negroes than whites (67 compared to 21 per cent), greater among Protestants than Catholics (32 compared to 15 per cent). Non-voting is also more prevalent in rural than in urban areas, more common among the very young people and the very old voters than those of middle age, and more common in the lower income and educational brackets than in the higher ones (Table 3.41).

By means of public opinion polls, we have learned the composition of the two major political parties. In general, Republicans are favored by older age groups, Protestants, farmers, the better-educated, the more respected occupants, and the higher-income brackets; and Democrats by the younger age groups, Catholics, city dwellers, the less-educated, laborers, and the lower-income brackets (Table 3.41). The Republican election victories in 1952 and 1956 showed that Negroes, Catholics, and wives of workers had to some extent switched party to vote for General Eisenhower. Kennedy's victory in 1960 was evidence that these categories had returned to their predominant Democratic allegiance. In general, one must remember that there is a large overlap in terms of background characteristics of supporters of the two parties. It is true that more Democrats are recruited from families headed by a member of a labor union, but the Republicans also have strength in this category – no less than 23 per cent of their support in 1952 came from members of families headed by a union man or woman (Table 3.41). Given such similar popular backing, the parties are hardly instruments of "class politics." While some issues divide them, their major difference is perhaps simply that they promote separate slates of persons for political office. The importance of the outwardly projected personal quality of the candidate for high political office is enhanced by the use of television and other mass media in making him known to the voters.

4. *Economy and Prosperity*

An outstanding fact about America and Americans is the near-worship of wealth. Any transaction called economic is one involving negotiable evaluations. For instance, "prices" are the evaluations given to goods; "fees" and "wages" are the evaluations given to services and labor. A measure of the *prosperity* of a society is its gross national product (GNP) which is the value of all the total output of goods and services in a year. In 1960, GNP passed the level of 500 billion dollars a year, and in 1964 it is pushing the 600 billion mark (Table 4.11). In all, the United States is not just barely the most prosperous nation in the world: it has 40.9 per cent of all income in the world (Table 4.10). Comparisons over time between any measures of prosperity must take into account changes in the unit of evaluation, that is, in the purchasing power of the dollar. Discounting inflation, the GNP has had a long-range average increase of about 2.9 per cent since 1900. Fluctuations are rather large: the 1948-53 average (which included the national effort of the Korean War) was 5.2 per cent, and the period 1953 to 1957 averaged 2.7 per cent of growth a year, while the average has been over 3 per cent since 1959. The 1960 election made the issue of growth of the GNP somewhat of a national concern; however, it may be a while before the politicians and the voters grasp the not-too-clear technical principles of economic growth and come to realize that the computation of GNP is very complex and subject to margins of error that make small, short-range changes in the figures rather meaningless. In general, growth is a function of investment, that is, money taken from consumers of wealth and channeled back to the producers of wealth. While statistics on these matters are subject to many a caveat, published reports indicate that in the United Kingdom, between 1950 and 1957, gross investment represented somewhat over 13 per cent of GNP and the annual rate of increase in GNP was below 3 per cent. In Mexico, the U.S., France, and Belgium, gross investment ran higher—between 16 per cent and 17 per cent of GNP; and in these countries GNP climbed at rates varying from just over 3 per cent to just over 5 per cent. In Japan, Venezuela, and the U.S.S.R., on the other hand, gross investment reached such expansive rates as 25 per cent to 29 per cent of GNP. And the growth of GNP speeded up accordingly, ranging up to 8 per cent rate in Japan and above 9 per cent in Venezuela.[11] Investments, in turn, occur when profitable opportunities are manifold; inventions that flow from research provide such opportunities, and so does a growing population and an increasing public concern for its welfare. Since these three factors are all expanding, the prospects are good that investments, and hence growth, will continue.

In the economy, we distinguish the *producers* of wealth (earners) from the *consumers* of wealth (spenders); between them stand the *dealers*. Of course, the same organization or person may, at different times, appear in all these capacities. The traditional American producer of wealth is

[11] "The U. S. Invents a New Way to Grow", *Business Week*, Special Report reprint from issue of January 23, 1960, p. 11.

usually pictured as a resourceful entrepreneur, and the traditional American consumer as a materialistically oriented sucker, avidly acquiring mechanical gadgets and capital goods from a fast-talking, not-too-honest salesman. Considerable correction is needed in all these images. The biggest producers of wealth are corporations with diffuse ownership directed by specialists in administration; the biggest consumers of wealth are the federal, state, and local governments; and the biggest dealers in wealth are professional investment managers.

In 1959, there were over a million corporations in the United States which filed balance sheets with their tax returns. The total book value of these corporations was 1,137 billion dollars (Table 4.30). They controlled about two-thirds of the national wealth, and their net income was 47 billion dollars. There were 7,000 corporations with assets over 50 million dollars. This 0.2 per cent of all corporations accounted for 62 per cent of all corporate income (Table 4.31). In some areas of manufacturing, a few companies dominate the market. Thus, in the field of motor vehicles, of motors and generators, of aircraft engines, of aircrafts, of structural steel, and of packed meat, four or fewer corporations employed one-half or more of all persons engaged in the industry.

Legally, the corporations are owned and operated by their shareholders. One out of six adult Americans owned common stock in 1962, while ten years earlier only one out of sixteen owned shares (Table 4.33). On the average, executives and directors own only one or two per cent of the outstanding shares of the large corporations. This separation of ownership and control was already well established in the 1920's. Recent practices tend to reverse this trend, or at least hold it in check. During the post-war years, it has become standard practice to remunerate executives, not merely in the form of high salaries, but also by offering them options to buy stock in the company they serve. A stock option plan usually states that certain executives, over their years of service to the company, shall have the right to buy a specified number of its shares at a price that is equal to or somewhat lower than the market price at time of their appointment, or at the time of the enactment of the option plan. While this practice involves the executives deeply in the growth of the company (and in the consequent appreciation of their option shares) it has not changed the fact that the vast majority of all common shares are held by "absentee" owners.

In effect, individual savers who buy stock in companies are estimated to contribute only about 5 per cent of the capital that flows into the non-agricultural industries. Some 20 per cent is borrowed from banks, and another 20 per cent comes from insurance companies and pension trusts. More than half of the new capital invested in American industries comes from undistributed profits, that is, depreciation allowances and retained earnings, that are plowed back into the company.[12] The latter figure suggests that the executives are keenly interested in the consolidation and

[12] Adolf A. Berle, Jr., *Power Without Property*, Harpers, New York, 1959, p. 45.

expansion of their companies, thereby consolidating and enhancing their own position of power and appreciating the value of their option shares. The traditional practice of turning all profit over to the shareholders is very rare. The shareholders do not object much about this; they pay a high income tax on their dividends but a lower capital gains tax on increases in the value of their equity in a company. Given this structure, changes in depreciation allowances are likely to have the most powerful and immediate impact on investment rates and hence on economic growth.

We mentioned that 20 per cent of capital entering American industry comes by a little known avenue, the investment staffs of insurance companies and pension trusts. This channel of capital movement is becoming increasingly important in the United States. In 1957-58, seventy-one per cent of all stockholdings (in terms of their dollar value) were held by individual Americans or American firms, and two per cent by foreigners. The balance—27 per cent—was in trusts and non-profit foundations, of which the insurance and pension funds are the most important (Table 4.32). These "institutional holdings" have expanded more rapidly than any other sector of the national prosperity. They represent riches that are *owned* neither by individuals, as in traditional capitalism, nor by the state, as in socialism, but *vested* in the hands of a rather small group of professional investment trustees. The investment trustees of various funds, and the executives in banks and corporations with similar functions, form a new category of middle men, whose activities place them between the producers of wealth and the consumers of wealth. In effect, they are the brokers and dealers in big money, and around them the American prosperity revolves.

The largest consumers of wealth are the national, state, and local governments which, during the past decade, have spent between a fifth and a quarter of the GNP. The costs and debts of state and local government have been increasing at a much faster rate than those of the federal government. The federal, state, and local governments in the last decade have spent more than they have received in revenues. While both parties subscribe to the idea of a budget balanced over the long run, the deficits in years of crisis generally exceed the surpluses in good years. In dollar volume, the market in government bonds and other instruments of its debt dwarfs the stock market better than ten to one. Municipal bonds are tax-exempt, which explains why they find a market among the wealthy.

The U.S. government spends about half of its revenue on defense. (This is more than all business profits in the land.) The government farms out most of its needs for military supplies and research to corporations; actually half of all money for prime military contracts goes to 25 leading corporations. The total defense cost is a little less than one tenth of the GNP, a proportion higher than most NATO countries. The Soviet Union spends about 20 per cent of its GNP on defense. Since its GNP is about half that of the U. S. figure, the actual amount spent on defense by these two powers is about the same. The over-riding question is which one spends it most wisely.

Perhaps a quarter of all the money the federal government collects in taxes from businesses goes back to business enterprises (including farms) in the form of subsidies. One study estimates the rise in direct federal subsidies from 1.9 billion in 1951 to 7.5 billions in 1960. Business mail is subsidized to the tune of half a billion dollars, and so is the transportation industry, particularly airlines and maritime companies. The largest recipient of federal subsidies is agriculture, which received .9 billion in 1951 and 3.6 billions in 1960.[13] If it were not for the human and political agony involved, the country could dispense with four-fifths of its smallest farms, and remaining big ones would produce enough food to feed the nation without the present rate of subsidies.

The prevailing sentiments favor increased investments in education, science and welfare. The federal government seems to be the only agency able and prepared to pay the lion's share of the added cost for these programs. Such additional federal expenditures for non-defense services will probably force some adjustments at the points where the body politic and the economy meet. Several adjustments to the increased federal spending are possible: one can have a gradual inflation which allows every debtor, and above all the government, to pay back in cheaper money than he borrowed; one can cut other government expenses (e.g. the subsidies for agriculture may be gradually abolished, or defense spendings may be reduced after an international arms control agreement is negotiated); or, one can increase the government income by levying higher taxes. Funds may also be forthcoming in a less painful way: by an increase in the general prosperity of the land at a faster pace than any increase in government expenditures. If so, one can add somewhat to the government's outlays without increasing its debt or boosting its tax rates — and still have the citizens more prosperous. An interesting experiment is to achieve this prosperity by the added investment that would follow a cut in taxes.

It should not be forgotten that public funds for research, education and welfare are to a considerable extent augmented from private sources. In the past decade, more private foundations were formed than ever before. One calculation from the late 1950's showed that 975 foundations had a capital of a million dollars or more (Table 4.40). The foundations in 1962 divided their giving so that education got 40 per cent, international activities 14 per cent, health institution 12 per cent, other social welfare programs 12 per cent, research 16 per cent, religious institutions 6 per cent (Table 4.41). Private citizens also have giving habits; it seems customary for the American family to give between 3 and 5 per cent of their income to charity.

Economic facts on the level of the household are easier to grasp. Most family income comes from salaries and wages. The American labor force almost tripled in size since 1890, thus expanding somewhat faster than did the population of working age. The number of women in the labor

[13] From a study of federal subsidy and subsidy-like programs by the Joint Economic Committee of Congress, reported in *The New York Times*, December 19, 1960, p. 38.

force rose by 505 per cent in this period, while the female population rose only 330 per cent (Table 4.50). In 1960, 32 per cent of the total labor force were females, of whom over half were married. To be gainfully employed is no longer a prerogative of the single woman or a reluctant necessity for the poor one: 61 per cent of the working women are married (Table 4.51). We have already mentioned that modern women, unlike their mothers, tend to marry young and have all their children during the span of a few years while they are in their twenties. They are still comparatively young when their children become old enough to take care of themselves, and the mothers are thus free to voluntarily enter the labor force and to spend many years working before retirement age. (In European countries with later marriage age, it is more common for women to have a career before marriage.)

The average work week is now some 25 hours shorter than a century ago. In 1960 it was 38 hours in factories and 44 hours on farms (Table 4.60). The most recent figures indicate – contrary to expectations – that the work week is increasing. Due to the heavy cost of fringe benefits, it seems cheaper for employers to offer their existing personnel overtime instead of hiring new workers. It may be mentioned that studies of executives in industry indicate that their actual work week is around 60 hours, the same as that of workers in the 1890's.

Every month the Bureau of the Census asks a representative sample of American households whether anyone in them now holds a job or is looking for a job. Those who answer that they are looking for a job are counted as "unemployed." This measure of unemployment is very generous, since housewives, teenagers, and retired people may at times be in the mood of looking and at times not; there is no social norm expecting them to work consistently, and many go in and out of the labor force, depending on personal emergencies and temptations. This subjective basis for American statistics on unemployment largely accounts for the fact that the U.S. figures of unemployment are usually higher than those of Western European countries. However, the U.S. figures since 1958 have been higher than five per cent of the labor force (Table 4.61). There are more unemployed persons in the United States than there are farmers. The future prospects for a long-range check on unemployment are somewhat dim. Increased mechanization and automation threaten many manual and clerical jobs. Particularly jobs demanding little skill – and hence often held by Negroes and Puerto Ricans – may disappear with automation, thus creating unemployment (Table 4.62). Further complications are added by the increasing cadres of teenagers and young adults that will enter the job market, and also the swelling number of wives who will be launching their children and be ready to go to work. Even if we allow for the fact that many more teenagers and adults than before will spend time in colleges rather than jobs, it seems likely that the labor force during the 60's will increase at rates over 2 per cent a year, or more than twice as fast as in the 50's. In all, some 50,000 new jobs have to be created every week to absorb the job-seekers. In the last few decades, it has been the practice of both Democratic and Republican administrations to use government powers to stem slumps in the labor market. A formal declaration in the Employment Act of 1946 states that "it is the continuing policy and responsibility of the federal government to use all practicable means . . . to promote maximum employment, production and purchasing power." This sentiment — although subject to some ideologically inspired opposition — is likely to prevail in the near future. Since the unemployed is a voter and often allied with a powerful labor bloc, we may expect increased government manipulation of the economy in the name of full employment.

The labor force is not merely increasing but is also changing in composition. The proportions engaged in agricultural and related fields and in private household service have shown a long-term decline, while there are slow increases in proportions engaged in manufacturing, transportation, and communications, and pronounced increases in the professional, managerial, and clerical groups and among operatives and kindred workers. One out of every nine economically active persons is now a professional or a technician. Of special significance is the decline in farmers and farm workers from over one-third of the economically active in 1900 to 6.3 per cent in 1960 (Table 4.53).

The variation in income from occupation to occupation is considerable (Table 4.70). More interesting are the shifts in the rates of gain. During the 1940's, semi-skilled factory workers increased their incomes by 172 per cent, while professional and managerial incomes rose 96 per cent. In the 1950's, however, the latters' income increased 75 per cent, while factory workers received a 59 per cent increase. In terms of money income, nearly one quarter of all families made less than $4,000, nearly one quarter made between $4,000 and $6,000, and more than half of all families made over $6,000. One out of 14 could be called well off, by virtue of having had a yearly income of more than $15,000 (Table 4.72). There was a considerable income differential between annual earnings of men and women, and between the white and non-white populations. Men earned three times as much as women (Table 4.71). White people earn about twice as much as Negroes. Actually, the relative earnings of Negroes are slipping. In 1939, the median male Negro worker earned 41 per cent of the median white wage. By 1950, the Negro earned 61 per cent of the corresponding white earnings. But by 1962, the Negro income had slipped to 55 per cent of the median white income. However, the constantly rising wages and salaries (both the actual and the inflationary portions) and the constantly improved consumer goods that wages can buy seem to give most Americans a feeling that they are "getting ahead." In reality, the chances for a worker to move into the middle class in the United States do not seem to be too different from those in other advanced countries. However, the likelihood of making a very long leap upward, from a working class home into the elite, is higher in the United States than in other countries (Table 4.55). The American dream is a reality – but not for everyone.

As consumers, we enjoy the prosperity of the nation. There has been a steady rise in the proportion of families who own their own homes. In 1960, 60 per cent of all families owned their homes, and the median value of their homes was $11,900. Nine out of 10 American homes had a television set. In consumer goods during the 1950's America was as rich as all the rest of the world combined (Table 4.84). Enormous effort goes into the enterprise of making the consumers absorb the abundance of goods produced by the American economy. To this end, a huge advertising and marketing system has emerged; and to a considerable extent, mass media, such as television, have become adjuncts to corporative marketing. If a time-and-motion study were made of all Americans, we should probably find an unprecedented amount of time and energy devoted to receiving information about consumer goods from mass media, and in comparing notes on consumer goods in conversation.

Buying on installment plans has become exceedingly frequent–half of all families have installment debts – and the amount of consumer debt has more than doubled in the last ten years. It has become common for the monthly re-payments of installment debts to absorb more than 10 per cent of the consumers' take-home pay; in 1963 the figure was 13.6 per cent. More people than ever can borrow money with comparative ease. It is now normal that heads of families are subject to semi-public credit ratings, and concern over one's credit standing may often be greater than the concern over one's saving account. This extensive consumer credit structure has many repercussions. It pre-supposes stable family incomes and is, in effect, one reason why the government and the business community endorse a policy of relatively full employment. The extensive use of credit in buying homes has also had a complicating effect on the labor market. People sometimes cannot move from a house in an area of high unemployment to an area with many jobs, because no one wants to buy their house and assume their mortgage obligations. When asked "What kinds of things do you worry about most?" 43 per cent mentioned personal financial problems. By contrast, 24 per cent mentioned health problems and 15 per cent international or national issues; clearly economic worries are the most prevalent.

In 1958-60, households spent 27 per cent of their income on food, 11 per cent on clothing and personal accessories, 27 per cent on the home and its furnishings. Six per cent was spent on recreation. No less than 12 per cent was spent on the family car and transportation. Medical and death expenses took 6.3 per cent of the income (Table 4.80). It is perhaps worth noting that expenditures on main items increase proportionately with increasing income. Households receiving under $2,000 in annual income and households receiving more than $10,000 spend 36 and 24 per cent respectively on food, 7 and 11 per cent on homes and furnishings, 5 and 6 per cent on recreation (Table 4.81). These small differences indicate the existence of a steeply graded series of consumer goods; good meat may cost three times more than standard meat, a fancy car four times more than the standard model, a mansion many times more than the prefabricated house, and so forth. Contrary to a great deal of popular talk about the deplorable extent of standardization in American life, these facts suggest considerable differentation between Americans. It is also worth noting that consumers now need fewer of their dollars to meet fixed expenses. Discretionary income, that is, what is left after fixed and essential expenses are met, has increased by 60 per cent since 1955. This allows for a personalized style of life.

Many protest movements against an uneven distribution of riches in society are recorded by historians. In its extreme form, a denial of its legitimacy takes the form of utopian socialism, the idea that everyone shall be given equal shares of the economic good. In practice, however, there seems to be no exception to the rule that class protests have served only to modify existing class divisions, or to replace one class division by another. In the United States socialist protests have been weak; a Socialist Labor Party participated in the elections of 1888 and 1896, and received in the latter year only 36,000 votes. In the depression election of 1932, the socialists polled 918,000 votes. This represents the strongest year in the recent record of the socialist movement in the United States; by 1936 their support had fallen to 197,000 votes. As the United States has grown more prosperous, the difference in income between the very rich and the very poor has largely remained what it used to be. Legal guarantees of a minimum wage and of old-age pensions reduce the number of the very poor, and progressive taxation and inheritance taxes check the accumulation of wealth among the rich. But there is no drastic redistribution of wealth.

Much existing discontent with one's economic position in the United States is channeled not into renewed efforts to improve one's lot through study or hard work, nor into political radicalism, but into — gambling. Gambling keeps alive the hope of a spectacular economic advancement. Since most gambling in the United States is illegal, we have no reliable figures showing how much money is wagered. However, most estimates agree that large sums are involved, perhaps as much as a few per cent of the GNP. A good share of this money is used to pay bribes to local authorities so that anti-gambling laws will not be enforced, and another good share is kept by the underworld syndicates that control illegal gambling. Some money is, of course, returned to the gambler, but at poor odds — just enough to keep his dream alive and his gambling habits active. The nation faces a difficult problem here. A modest amount of gambling may be an antidote to economic frustrations which, if allowed to run their course, might destroy the present political and economic system. Yet it is an outrage that this antidote is administered in doses that make for addiction and that it is administered by underworld syndicates. However, government control or licensing of the gambling industry, channelling the

"the take" to the U.S. Treasury and non-profit accounts used for the public good, is at best partial. Somehow, such use of gambling is contrary both to the American ideology of private enterprise and to the American puritanism which abhors the thought that the state should implicitly encourage establishments of gambling. As a social problem in the United States, gambling ranks second only to race relations.

5. *Science and Knowledge*

A distinguishing fact about modern society is its enormous effort to develop new *knowledge*. The United States is participating vigorously in this trend. The launching of the first Soviet sputnik was not only a scientific triumph; it was an event that shaped public opinion into renewed support of American science. Funds for research and development from all sources doubled between 1955 and 1960 and may double again before the end of 1965. The federal government foots roughly two thirds of the national bill for research. The largest item in the federal research budget—a sizable sum indeed—is simply for a trip to the moon. Almost 10 per cent of all research funds—or an estimated 1.3 billion dollars in 1961—was spent on basic research, that is, research with no other immediate purpose than to widen knowledge (Table 5.20). Most government money went into the physical sciences. The big foundations used to give most of their support to the social sciences, but now they give more to the physical sciences (Table 4.41).

The traditional measure of new knowledge is the number of scholarly publications that appear. Here the picture for the United States is not encouraging, partly because of a failure by publishers to issue scholarly books with small editions. The U.S. figure is barely above that of France and much below the figure for the Soviet Union (Table 5.11). In fact, the number of American scientific books hardly increased at all between 1938 and 1958, in spite of the increase in scientific facilities. Since that time, the number of scholarly books—particularly in the social sciences—has increased rapidly (Table 5.10). Although scientific journals have grown in number and scope, there can be no doubt that findings by American scientists are slow in reaching print, a fact that retards the spread of knowledge and makes the achievement of new knowledge more difficult.

The scientific effort is also reflected in the number of persons who produce new knowledge, the *scholars*, the number who transmit it to others, the *teachers*, and in the number who receive it, the *students*. Presumably, the number of people who obtain a doctor's degree (the Ph.D. degree, the Ed.D., or the Sc.D.) stands for at least that many contributions to science, in the form of their doctoral theses. At the turn of the century, the number of such doctorates annually was about 250; now it is over 12,000. The number of living holders of doctor's degrees in the physical and biological sciences has more or less doubled in every decade since 1900. To this latter should be added the working scientists who do not have doctorates, a group estimated to be 6 or 7 times larger.[14] Most of those who achieve doctorates continue to contribute to further growth of scientific knowledge. A study has shown that during the first eight or nine years after receiving their doctorates, eight out of ten natural scientists have published at least one title other than their dissertation. The corresponding figures for Ph.D.s in psychology is seven out of ten, in mathematics and English, six out of ten, and in history, two out of ten.[15]

The number of teachers is now counted in the millions (Table 5.30). One out of every five teachers in the United States is a college teacher. In terms of training, community standing, and to some extent also in terms of the age groups they instruct, American college professors are the counterparts of the senior teachers in gymnasiums and lycees on the European continent. The universities proper – that is, colleges with graduate schools – number around 200. The following ten were rated as the very best by a study done in 1957: Harvard, California (Berkeley), Columbia, Yale, Michigan, Chicago, Princeton, Wisconsin, Cornell, and Illinois. This rating did not include the engineering schools; if Massachusetts Institute of Technology and California Institute of Technology are added to this list, we have a group of twelve outstanding universities which awarded one third of all doctor's degrees in 1957-58.[16]

Most elementary and secondary schools are public – the private ones are mostly Catholic parochial schools – but among the schools for higher learning there are more private than public ones. Since public schools are operated by the local, rather than national government, school budgets become important issues in local politics, and the school curriculum is not immune to influence from local figures of power or money. This situation is rather different from the typical European one in which schools are run by a ministry of education and subject to the influence of national politics and national figures of power. Whether increased federal aid to education will move the American system toward the European pattern is a matter of debate at present.

A small group of private boarding schools for boys has a unique position of prestige in the United States. Sometimes known as St. Grottlesex, they comprise these schools: St. Paul's, St. Mark's, Groton, St. George's, Kent, Exeter, and Middlesex. These schools are the nearest correspondence on the American scene to famous "public" schools like Eton and Harrow in England; they have a social as well as academic significance. While many additional secondary schools in the United States have an academic excellence that equals or excells St. Grottlesex, the over-all quality is not all encouraging. At the turn of the century, more than half of the high school students studied algebra, but in the 1950's only a quarter took algebra.

Americans nowadays remain longer in their schools in more senses than one. The average length of the school year increased from 144 days

[14] Dael Wolfle, *America's Resources of Specialized Talent,* Harpers, New York, 1954, p. 41.

[15] Bernard Berelson, *Graduate Education in the United States,* McGraw-Hill, New York, 1960, p. 55.

[16] *Ibid.* p. 126.

in 1900 to 178 days in 1960 (Table 5.31). The per cent enrolled in schools has increased in every age and stratum, and educational attainment has increased too; at the beginning of this century the average American completed elementary school, while now he completes high school and increasingly often goes on to college. The relative size of the college population in the United States is far above that of any other country for which we have statistics. In the year 1900, one youth out of every sixty reaching the age 22 had been graduated from college. The corresponding figure for 1963 is one out of eight, and it may be one out of four before long. In 1900, nearly half of all college graduates had prepared themselves for law, medicine, or the ministry, professions which only one out of fifteen recent graduates enter. The college graduate today is more likely to continue his training in a school of business or a school of education than in the traditional fields of medicine, law, and the ministry.

While the average schooling of the American is longer than that of the average subject of any foreign country for which we have information, other ways of telling how educated the nation is may show a different picture. For example, in 1957, pollsters in several countries got together to check how many persons were currently reading a book. In England no less than 55 per cent were found reading a book, in West Germany 34 per cent, in Australia 33 per cent, Canada 31 per cent, and in the United States—17 per cent. The low American figure is in part explained by the comparatively few genuine bookstores found in the United States.

The indices we have of *competence,* that is, command of knowledge, are based on examinations and educational diplomas and degrees. The ladder of degrees is in theory a fairly clear-cut measure, in the sense that the holder of a higher degree usually knows more than the holder of a lower degree. Six regional accreditation boards concentrate on setting standards for colleges, in order that degrees from different accredited colleges may be as nearly as possible equal in the competence they imply. There are similar checks made, in the various states, of grammar schools and high schools. However, the local or private control of education in the United States cannot but cause considerable variation in the meaning of degrees and diplomas. There are many who believe that Americans are becoming increasingly conscious of degrees and diplomas, but the great variations in the meaning of the same degree from one school to another and from one decade to another make snobbism about degrees a tenuous enterprise.

Academic competence has not been equally distributed among all categories of the population. In 1900, over two-thirds of all college graduates were men, and even at mid-century men outnumbered women three to two. The education of the Negro population has posed special problems for the United States. Fewer Negroes receive a higher education, but the difference between the races is declining. In the population over 65, the non-whites have only half the amount of schooling of the whites, a fact that reflects what used to be. In the age group 25 to 29, however, the non-whites have nine-tenths of the schooling of the whites, as measured in years of education; and this reflects the recently achieved near-equality (Table 5.55). Still, white students make better progress in school than Negro students; the typical Negro is about a year behind his age group in terms of his grade level.

It is not surprising that persons in higher income and occupational groups have higher education. In 1959, farm laborers had a median schooling of 8 years, and other laborers had 9 years. Farmers, too, had a median education of 9 years, a fact, incidentally, indicating that they will not get the better city jobs should they abandon their farms. Operatives, craftsmen, and service workers have 10 or 11 years of education, salesmen and clerks 13 years, managers, officials and proprietors have a median education of 12 years, and professionals and semiprofessionals over 16 years (Table 5.61). We also know that Protestants and Jews have, on balance, more education than Catholics (Table 6.3).

Very roughly speaking, college graduates earn twice as much money as high school graduates, and high school graduates earn twice the amount of those who have only elementary school (Table 5.60). Since most jobs now are salaried and cannot be passed on to children like property, those who hold privileged positions in society have to send their children to college in order to maintain their family's position (Table 5.51).

The expansion of college education has, on the whole, reduced the educational inequalities in terms of sex, race, religion, and income, but it has at the same time increased the inequalities in terms of age. The expanded facilities for higher education have been opened primarily to young people. In response to this inequality, colleges for adults have emerged. In 1950, under the influx of veterans from World War II, 5.4 per cent of the men in the 25-29 age-group, a category clearly over-aged for conventional colleges, were engaged in undergraduate education in New York City.[17] The veterans are no longer in school, but the colleges for adults have maintained or enlarged their enrollments; one per cent of all adults say that they went to a lecture or adult school "yesterday" (Table 7.3).

6. *Religion and Sacredness*

It is easier to sketch the order, prosperity, and knowledge of a country by means of statistics than to picture its concern with religion, art, and ethics. Figures are not only scarcer in the latter fields; they are also in greater need of supplementation by facts of a non-quantitative kind.

Our prosperity seems to grow almost constantly; new knowledge is created every day; and additions to the social order are made in every season. In religion, the picture is more static: new forms of sacredness appear rarely on the American scene. In the last century, American Protestantism has witnessed only a few new forms of religious life—

[17] 1950 Census of Population, vol. 2, Part 32, *New York*, Washington, D.C., 1952, p. 235 and p. 220.

Mormonism is perhaps the best known — and American Catholicism has seen only two of its representatives becoming beatified by the Roman Catholic Church. The religious emphasis in America — as indeed in most modern countries — is to transmit the religious heritage from generation to generation, not to add to it. If anything, it appears as if American Christianity in this process is subtracting several items from its heritage to make it more consonant with modern tastes. There are certain signs indicating that religion in America has lost some of its theological salinity. From 1905 to 1940, the proportion of articles about religion in popular magazines declined two-thirds; this holds for articles on religious dogma, for instance, the after-life, atonement, baptism, and the devil, as well as articles on church work. However, the number of articles on topics like the relation of religion to politics, to economy, and to science increased. The decline of interest in dogma is also evident in a comparative analysis of hymns used in 1836 and in 1939: it was found that hymns on traditional dogmas decreased from 45 to 12 per cent of the total.[18] A certain ignorance about the Bible is also evident in the United States; only 35 per cent of adult Americans could name the four gospels, whereas in a poll in Great Britain 61 per cent got this answer right (Table 6.10). Perhaps the fact that religion is not taught in most American schools accounts for much of the scriptural illiteracy; the clergy apparently find it easier to talk to the American laity about getting along with neighbors and colleagues and about civic and economic responsibilities than about the Atonement, the Law, the Sacraments, and other central religious aspects.

However, more Americans belong to a church today than at any previous time; the proportion of the population named on a church roll increased from one sixth in the 1850s to two thirds in the 1960s. Another index of the organizational trends in religion in the United States is the change in the number of clergymen. In the past fifty years they have increased by more than two thirds. However, the population has more than doubled in the same period, so that the number of clergymen per person has actually declined. Whether there has been any change in church participation during this period is impossible to ascertain; we obtained no data before 1939, and the samplings taken since then were not taken at the same time of the year. At mid-century the Catholics reported that 62 per cent were attending mass on Sundays and holy days (an obligation which it is a serious sin to evade); of the Protestants 25 per cent were present at church every Sunday, and of the Jews 12 per cent attended synagogue every Saturday.[19] By international standards these are high figures; certainly they are not matched by the other Western countries for which we have data.

A sample census in 1957 gave us, for the first time, uniform information as to how Americans from age 14 up describe their religious affiliations or backgrounds (Table 6.20). It showed the United States as being

[18] Michael Argyle, *Religious Behavior,* Free Press, Glencoe, 1959, pp. 32-33.
[19] Thomas Ford Hoult, *The Sociology of Religion,* Dryden Press, New York, 1958, p. 107.

two-thirds (66.2 per cent) Protestant and a quarter (25.7 per cent) Roman Catholic; the Jewish faith was reported by 3.2 per cent, other religions by 1.3 per cent, and no religion by 2.7 per cent. The remaining one per cent did not report their religion – a small proportion, considering the fact that the question was answered on a voluntary basis. The Catholics are over-represented in urban areas, as are, to an even greater extent, the Jews. The largest of the Protestant denominations are the Baptists (29.8 per cent of all Protestants), the Methodists (21.1 per cent), the Lutherans (10.7 per cent), and the Presbyterians (8.4 per cent).

From other sample surveys we know the relative educational and economic achievements of adherents to the various Protestant denominations. We find, for example, that 35 per cent of Baptists (many of whom are Negroes), 44 per cent of Lutherans, 51 per cent of Methodists, 63 per cent of Presbyterians, and 71 per cent of Congregationalists have been graduated from high school. The corresponding figure for Catholics is 43 per cent, and for Jews 63 per cent (Table 6.30).

Popular and scholarly discussions often depict religion as a conservative force in America. However, it is unwise to generalize on this point. For example, Negro ministers seem more often champions of racial integration of the schools than are the Negro teachers.

7. *Art and Beauty*

Basic sociological facts about art in America are insufficient and incomplete. It is rather idle to ask how many works of lasting beauty are created in America. However, every day some 180 new musical compositions and 45 books of fiction are copyrighted. Paintings are not subject to this kind of numeration, but it is perhaps not unreasonable to assume that the United States in recent years has been the birthplace for the largest number of the world's abstract paintings.

New York is a great center for all forms of fine art. It is the American Mecca for publishing, music, dance, and theatre. It has probably more art galleries than Paris. Chicago and San Francisco also maintain a significant share in the nation's artistic life. Most big American cities have an art museum – there are over 200 all told – and about a dozen cities have symphony orchestras in residence, but there are many big cities without a permanent stage company. Believe it or not, twice as many Americans (37 million) seem to attend concerts and recitals as the number who see major league baseball, the national sport. Some 41 million (many school children) pass the turnstiles of museums and galleries, and some 9 million tickets to professional theater events are bought every year.[20]

We have some information about the number of people who report an artistic pursuit as a full-time occupation. The 1960 Census records 2 actors, 15 artists (or art teachers), 3 dancers (or dance teachers), and 27 musicians (or music teachers) per 10,000 persons in the experienced

[20] Estimates by Arnold Mitchell, Stanford Research Institute.

civilian labor force. These are modest figures. Moreover they are not increasing as fast as the labor force, and certainly not as fast as the professions. The number of recruits to artistic careers was higher in the 1940s than in the 1950s (Table 7.10).

Serious American artists normally have great difficulties in securing a decent livelihood from their art. For example, a study of fairly well established painters showed that the majority earned less than $500 a year from their art (Table 7.20). Nor do the artists have much control of decisions affecting art on the national or community level. An artist is unlikely to be on the board of directors of a museum or of an art center. Decisions affecting these art organizations are usually made by benefactors or professional art directors. Nor do the serious artists have much say in the design of consumer goods. The close relation and overlap found in, say, the Scandinavian countries between serious artists and industrial designers is unknown in America. A decisive influence on industrial design of consumer goods is instead exercised by market researchers who tend to recommend designs according to their often vulgar understanding of psychology, and who operate in an economic environment in which it is safer to underestimate than to overestimate popular taste.

Television has supplanted the radio and the film as the most popular medium of popular culture. As mentioned, it reaches almost every home, and the average TV-set was turned on over 5 hours per day. An American over twelve years of age spent an average of 120 minutes a day in 1958 watching television. This compares with 72 minutes of listening to the radio, 28 minutes reading the newspaper, and 14 minutes reading magazines.[21] Since the artistic quality of TV-programs is generally low, the many hours spent by Americans watching television is a source of concern (and challenge) to many intellectuals. Perhaps these figures should also be a source of concern to some of the makers of consumer goods whose advertising pays for the programs: the many hours of TV-watching often equals hours in which their goods and services are unused. One may doubt that, in the long run, sales of automobiles, gasoline, and some other products is promoted by keeping people idle in front of their TV-sets.

8. *Ethics and Virtue*

No account of America can bypass the topic of American morality. It is neither unusual nor ridiculous for an American to do good and try to be good. The United States is also, as should be evident from the preceding pages, a very heterogeneous nation, its people widely differentiated as to national origin, race, income, style of life, education, power, and religion. Still, most observers of the United States find in all segments of American society an amazing degree of consensus on moral values, amounting in fact to an "American ethos." This has two components. The first is an unusually explicit version of the humane ideals of Western civilization based upon

[21] Information furnished by Sindlinger and Co., Philadelphia.

Athenian philosophy, Roman law, and the Judeo-Christian tradition. It is a creed stressing the dignity of man and his inalienable rights of freedom and equality. It was written into the Declaration of Independence, the Preamble of the Constitution, the Bill of Rights; it has been articulated in innumerable sermons, in an untold number of classroom homilies, in almost every major presidential address; it is continually reiterated by politicians, by courts of justice, by editorial writers, and by almost every speaker addressing a voluntary association in America. Millions of immigrants have had to learn it; they are in fact formally examined on it prior to receiving American citizenship. (This prerequisite indeed gives a unique overtone to American citizenship: it is an achievement rather than a birthright. One cannot understand the peculiar force of the emotionally loaded notion, "un-American" in public discussions unless one takes into account the fact that being an "American" in this sense presupposes an adherence to the American creed that is not taken for granted in advance of proof.) The second component in the American ethos is patriotism. The Second World War and the ensuing Cold War have kept patriotism in the forefront of American values. The large veterans' organizations are its most visible self-appointed guardians, but it really embraces every segment of the nation. Even the smallest town arranges a Fourth of July Parade to reinforce it.

We do not have an adequate measure of the extent and intensity of belief in the American creed. An opinion poll took as its starting point a delicate border territory between the two components of the American ethos, that is, liberty and patriotism. It used a scale indicating willingness to give the right of free speech to Communists, critics of religion, advocates of nationalization of industry. This scale reveals great variations in tolerance between middle-class and working-class persons, and between well educated and less educated persons. It calls "more tolerant," 66 per cent of the college graduates, 42 per cent of the high school graduates, and 22 per cent of the grammar school graduates. A significant fact is that leaders of communities and influential voluntary associations are much more tolerant than the average citizen or rank-and-file member (Table 8.10).

A difficult test case for the American creed of equality and freedom is posed by the question of racial integration. The Negro protest against discrimination and in favor of equal opportunities is loud and clear; no less than 40 per cent of the Negroes said in 1963 that they had taken part in a sit-in, marched in a mass-protest, or picketed a segregated store or facility.[22] As a result, the attitudes of the white population is actually shifting a great deal, and the shift is rather fast. In 1963, a poll found 80 per cent of the whites speaking in favor of legal guarantees for equal job opportunities for Negroes, 91 per cent in favor of legal guarantees for equal rights for Negroes to use busses and trains, and 75 per cent spoke in favor of legal rights to integrated schooling. By contrast, in 1942, a poll showed that only 44 per cent of the whites interviewed favored integration on public trans-

[22] Poll of 1157 Negroes by Louis Harris for *Newsweek*, July 29, 1963.

portation facilities, and only 30 per cent agreed that white and Negro children should go to the same school. The gain in the South since 1942 has been most pronounced: in 1942 only 2 per cent spoke in favor of school integration, in 1956 14 per cent did, in 1963 43 per cent did; also, the proportion of white Southerners approving integration on streetcars and busses rose between those years from 4 to 80 per cent.[23] A small study of a Southern county indicates a greater readiness to desegregate in higher educational, income and occupational brackets than in lower ones (Table 8.20).

There is no national plan or legislation for desegregation. Precise ways of arranging the desegregation have not been specified by the courts. The last five years have seen a great deal of experimentation with different methods of desegregation, the legality of which have been subject to many reviews. The initiative belongs to the various competing protest groups, which take cases to court. A recurrent issue in the civil rights bills debated in Congress is the extent to which the Department of Justice shall be given the initiative. Most of the attempted methods achieve a so-called "token" integration, that is, normally one to three Negro students per 100 white students. The Negroes, however, are not very satisfied with token integration. A poll in 1963 showed that 66 per cent of all Negroes want to live in mixed neighborhoods with whites; 42 per cent of all Negroes living in the South say they would rather live in the North; 75 per cent would prefer to work alongside whites at their jobs, and 71 per cent would like their children to go to school with white children.[24] The problem is not only a legal and a moral one but also one of quality of training. The years of separate education for the races have also been years of unequal education and training.

In the case of Negro-white integration in residence, transportation, and schools, our data do not exhibit the consensus and the national unity assoicated with the American ethos. As was the case a hundred years ago at the time of the Civil War, the nation is divided. But the ideas of freedom and equality and patriotism are invoked with equal fervor by both sides. Thus, while advocates of opposing positions devote their energies to arguing that their particiular stand is the only one consistent with this moral heritage, the American ethos itself remains intact.

9. *Community: Local and National*

In the old days one could pretty much account for what happened to a person by knowing the events that took place within the boundaries of his village. Today the scope of the American "community," in the sense of all that we need to know in order to understand what happens to an American, is enormously larger. The once dominating rural community has

[23] Poll of 1260 white Americans by Louis Harris for *Newsweek,* October 21, 1963, compared with earlier data reported in Herbert H. Hyman and Paul B. Sheatsley, "Attitude Toward Desegregation," *Scientific American,* vol. 195, Number 6, December 1956, pp. 36-37.

[24] *Newsweek* poll, July 23, 1959, *op. cit.*

given way not merely to the urban community, but to the metropolitan community; in 1960, 63 per cent of the American population had become dwellers in large cities and suburban areas, the so-called "standard metropolitan areas" (Table 9.14). Half of the national population growth occurs in suburbs, that is, within the metropolitan area but outside the central cities. Life in suburbs was once a privilege for relatively well-off families, but the suburbs built after World War II were planned to suit the great masses. Houses in any one suburban neighborhood are alike in appearance, and price; and they appeal to rather specific income brackets. Hence, each income class tends to live in a kind of residential segregation. Since no immediate neighbor is much better off, class envy is kept at a minimum. Instead, a friendly competition is waged with one's neighbors in terms of consumer goods, gardening, participation in voluntary associations, charity contributions, et cetera; a competition in which no one has any great initial advantages or handicap. A part of this pattern is that Americans may be likely to move to another neighborhood if their income improves beyond the typical range in their present neighborhood.

The suburban life, of course, presupposes that the husband commutes (usually by car) to nearby cities or industrial sites. This means not only that the suburbs are void of menfolk during most of the day, but, more important, that family income is likely to be earned in one municipality and be spent in another. This system puts considerable strain on local self-government and municipal finance. More strain can be expected if the forecast comes true that suburban developments will make one almost continuous built-up area from Boston to Washington (a "megalopolis"). It is also significant that many of the standard metropolitan areas cut across the old lines between the states. (See the starred areas on the adjoining map.) It is perhaps conceivable that in the future the traditional divisions of states and counties will become mostly historical and sentimental divisions with which people identify, and that the effective administrative units will become larger and have borders embracing areas whose problems require a common solution.

Thus, as the city with its hinterland succeeded the rural village as the dominating American community, so even larger units are succeeding. The days are gone when one could hope to know America by studying its Middletown. Today events in Pittsburgh may have as much effect in Detroit as in Pittsburgh, and events in New York may have as much effect in Chicago or Los Angeles as in New York. An interdependent national community has developed. A greater share of the important decisions and issues have become national ones. Even the machinery for developing the knowledge on which decisions and debates are based has broken its local molds and become national. Writing in 1947, Robert S. Allen noted that in the preceding two decades 1,000 daily newspapers had disappeared, and that six large chains of newspapers controlled about half of the country's daily circulation.[25] The similar concentration of radio and TV stations into a few national networks is well known.

[25] Robert S. Allen, *Our Fair City*, Vanguard Press, New York, 1947, pp. 12-13.

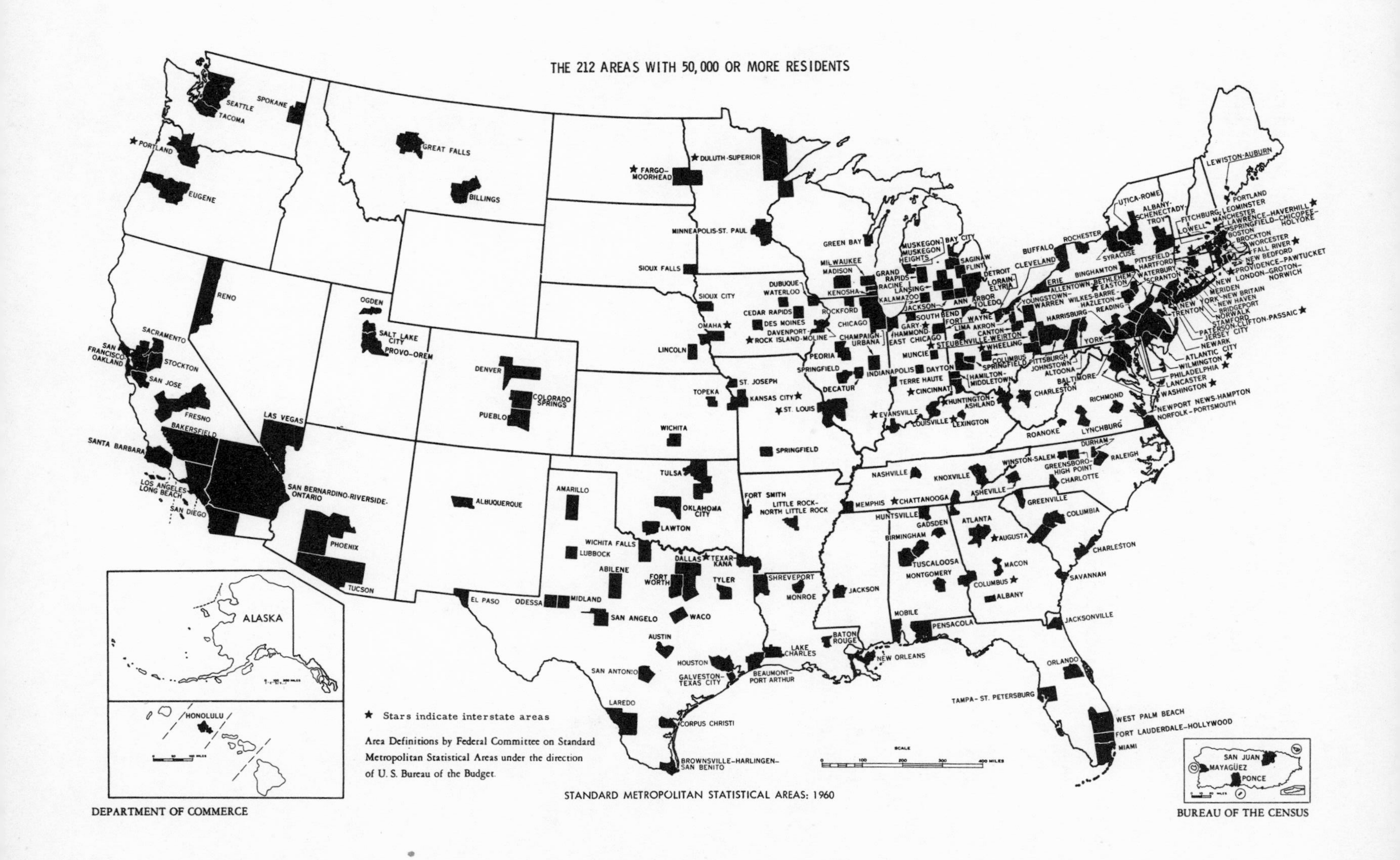
THE 212 AREAS WITH 50,000 OR MORE RESIDENTS
SEATTLE
TACOMA
SPOKANE
PORTLAND
EUGENE
GREAT FALLS
BILLINGS
FARGO-MOORHEAD
DULUTH-SUPERIOR
MINNEAPOLIS-ST. PAUL
SIOUX FALLS
SIOUX CITY
OMAHA
LINCOLN
RENO
SACRAMENTO
SAN FRANCISCO-OAKLAND
STOCKTON
SAN JOSE
FRESNO
BAKERSFIELD
SANTA BARBARA
LOS ANGELES-LONG BEACH
SAN DIEGO
SAN BERNARDINO-RIVERSIDE-ONTARIO
LAS VEGAS
PHOENIX
TUCSON
OGDEN
SALT LAKE CITY
PROVO-OREM
DENVER
COLORADO SPRINGS
PUEBLO
ALBUQUERQUE
EL PASO
ODESSA
MIDLAND
SAN ANGELO
AMARILLO
LUBBOCK
WICHITA FALLS
ABILENE
FORT WORTH
DALLAS
TEXARKANA
TYLER
WACO
AUSTIN
SAN ANTONIO
HOUSTON
GALVESTON-TEXAS CITY
BEAUMONT-PORT ARTHUR
LAKE CHARLES
LAREDO
CORPUS CHRISTI
BROWNSVILLE-HARLINGEN-SAN BENITO
TOPEKA
ST. JOSEPH
KANSAS CITY
WICHITA
TULSA
OKLAHOMA CITY
LAWTON
FORT SMITH
LITTLE ROCK-NORTH LITTLE ROCK
SHREVEPORT
MONROE
JACKSON
BATON ROUGE
NEW ORLEANS
ST. LOUIS
SPRINGFIELD
DUBUQUE
WATERLOO
CEDAR RAPIDS
DES MOINES
DAVENPORT-ROCK ISLAND-MOLINE
PEORIA
SPRINGFIELD
DECATUR
CHAMPAIGN-URBANA
ROCKFORD
CHICAGO
GREEN BAY
MILWAUKEE
MADISON
KENOSHA
RACINE
GARY-HAMMOND-EAST CHICAGO
SOUTH BEND
FORT WAYNE
MUNCIE
INDIANAPOLIS
TERRE HAUTE
EVANSVILLE
LOUISVILLE
LEXINGTON
CINCINNATI
HAMILTON-MIDDLETOWN
DAYTON
SPRINGFIELD
COLUMBUS
LIMA
AKRON
CANTON
TOLEDO
LORAIN-ELYRIA
CLEVELAND
YOUNGSTOWN-WARREN
STEUBENVILLE-WEIRTON
WHEELING
HUNTINGTON-ASHLAND
CHARLESTON
MUSKEGON-MUSKEGON HEIGHTS
GRAND RAPIDS
KALAMAZOO
LANSING
JACKSON
ANN ARBOR
DETROIT
FLINT
SAGINAW
BAY CITY
BUFFALO
ROCHESTER
SYRACUSE
UTICA-ROME
ALBANY-SCHENECTADY-TROY
BINGHAMTON
ERIE
PITTSBURGH
JOHNSTOWN
ALTOONA
HARRISBURG
YORK
LANCASTER
READING
ALLENTOWN-BETHLEHEM-EASTON
WILKES-BARRE-HAZLETON
SCRANTON
PHILADELPHIA
TRENTON
ATLANTIC CITY
WILMINGTON
BALTIMORE
WASHINGTON
NEW YORK
NEWARK
JERSEY CITY
PATERSON-CLIFTON-PASSAIC
STAMFORD
NORWALK
BRIDGEPORT
NEW HAVEN
NEW BRITAIN
MERIDEN
WATERBURY
HARTFORD
PITTSFIELD
NEW LONDON-GROTON-NORWICH
PROVIDENCE-PAWTUCKET
NEW BEDFORD
FALL RIVER
BROCKTON
WORCESTER
BOSTON
SPRINGFIELD-CHICOPEE-HOLYOKE
LAWRENCE-HAVERHILL
LOWELL
MANCHESTER
FITCHBURG-LEOMINSTER
PORTLAND
LEWISTON-AUBURN
RICHMOND
NEWPORT NEWS-HAMPTON
NORFOLK-PORTSMOUTH
ROANOKE
LYNCHBURG
DURHAM
RALEIGH
WINSTON-SALEM
GREENSBORO-HIGH POINT
CHARLOTTE
ASHEVILLE
KNOXVILLE
NASHVILLE
CHATTANOOGA
MEMPHIS
HUNTSVILLE
GADSDEN
BIRMINGHAM
TUSCALOOSA
MONTGOMERY
MOBILE
PENSACOLA
ATLANTA
AUGUSTA
MACON
COLUMBUS
ALBANY
GREENVILLE
COLUMBIA
CHARLESTON
SAVANNAH
JACKSONVILLE
ORLANDO
TAMPA-ST. PETERSBURG
WEST PALM BEACH
FORT LAUDERDALE-HOLLYWOOD
MIAMI
ALASKA
HONOLULU
SAN JUAN
MAYAGÜEZ
PONCE
SCALE
0 100 200 300 400 MILES
★ Stars indicate interstate areas
Area Definitions by Federal Committee on Standard Metropolitan Statistical Areas under the direction of U. S. Bureau of the Budget.
STANDARD METROPOLITAN STATISTICAL AREAS: 1960
DEPARTMENT OF COMMERCE
BUREAU OF THE CENSUS

The emerging national community is not merely united by adherence to the common American creed of patriotism, equality and freedom. Most Americans can name a relative, a former classmate, or a neighbor who is in a very different walk of life: someone who is very rich or someone who is very poor, someone of a different religious denomination, someone with a different party affiliation, someone in the West, someone in the South, someone in private business, someone in government service, someone who belongs to a union, someone who pursues an artistic career, etc. Almost everybody is part of the nationwide network of personal or family bonds spanning the social structure. The exact extent of this phenomenon, strangely enough, has not yet been studied to the point where it can be shown in a statistical table, but there is evidence enough to warrant the assumption that these bonds of personal and family loyalty serve to tie the complex national community together.

The multitude of links that the modern American seems to have with others who are different from him also serve to restrain him from being too partisan. The wide spread represented by an individual's numerous loyalties to different persons is perhaps the basis in the social structure for the strong desire to "get along" with people, a dominant character trait of the American of today.

THE ORGANIZATION OF A SOCIOLOGICAL ALMANAC

One should not pretend that there is complete agreement among social scientists as to the most relevant information that enters into a routine description of a society. However, as a rule, sociologists and historians, in dealing with total societies, begin by discussing:

1. Human resources
2. Material resources

Then they may proceed along many paths, but in the end they have usually described six interrelated but different realms of society. The latter are:

3. Polity
4. Economy
5. Science
6. Religion
7. Art
8. Ethics

Each of these realms has a dominant concern, that might be called its "institutional value." In polity it is *order*, in economy *prosperity*, in science *knowledge*, in religion *sacredness*, in art *beauty*, and in ethics it is *virtue*. In each of the institutional realms, descriptive sociology collects information about (a) the amount of institutional values; (b) the suppliers, purveyors, and receivers of the institutional values; (c) the stratification of the population according to their control over institutional values; and, when relevant, (d) information about social movements attempting to change the distribution of the institutional values. We shall proceed by these four items in some detail for the first three institutional realms, recording information according to the following schema:

	(a)		(b)		(c)
Institutional Realm	*Institutional Value*	*Supplier*	*Purveyor* of *Institutional Values*	*Receiver*	*Mode of Stratification*
Polity	Order	Ruler	Administrator	Subject	Power
Economy	Prosperity	Producer	Dealer	Consumer	Riches
Science	Knowledge	Scholar	Teacher	Student	Competence

In turning to the remaining realms of religion, art, and ethics, we cannot give the corresponding information in the same quantitative detail and will, therefore, at this time make far briefer notes that do not lend themselves to this organization. Finally (9), having dissected the society into these parts, we have to give attention to how they are integrated into an ongoing whole.

The tables of this almanac are numbered according to the above scheme. Thus, any table with a prefix '6.' will deal with religion, any table with the prefix '4.' will deal with the economy, et cetera. The same holds for the subheadings of the text.[1] The second and third digits have no special meaning at this time.[2]

H.L.Z.

[1] A rationale for this version of sociological taxonomy has been given in Hans L. Zetterberg, *Social Theory and Social Practice*, The Bedminster Press, New York, 1962, pp. 49-73.

[2] The work continues, however, on the development of a general schema to catalogue sociological tables assigning definite meanings also to the latter digits.

HOW TO READ A TABLE

Numbers in tables are important, not in their own right, but because they quantify a category that is important. This may appear so obvious that it seems unnecessary to point it out. Yet it is a common failing in reading a table to spend too little time becoming familiar with its framework of categories and their relation to each other. On the face of it, it seems more advantageous to look at these parts of a table before looking at the numbers, but whether before or after, it is always necessary to know and understand the kinds of things the numbers refer to before attempting to interpret a table.

The headings of a table include not only the various categories contained in the table but also the relation of these categories to each other. This relation cannot be grasped unless the meanings of the categories are clear. To facilitate understanding, definitions have been included in the tables in certain cases. The meanings of the categories are clear. The meanings of such categories as white, Negro, Protestant, Catholic, skilled worker, and unskilled worker are regarded as being generally understood, and such terms have not been defined (though there is no denying that it is necessary at times to be more explicit and precise about the meaning of even such commonly accepted categories). However, there are concepts which are not generally understood, or which are applied in a different sense from that of general usage, or which have changed in meaning over time. For example, the term "standard metropolitan area" is not generally familiar, and the meaning of "eligible" voter has changed over time. Therefore, each of these terms has been defind in footnotes. Careful reading of these footnotes is essential to the proper interpretation of the tables. To illustrate: since the criteria of electoral eligibility have changed over time, the ratio of the eligible population to the total population also changed (see table 3.40). Unless the changes in the criteria of eligibility were specified, the changes in this ratio could be misinterpreted.

In every table the numbers and categories refer to a specific population. A population is specified by indicating place and date, for example, U. S., 1900; India, 1961. There may be further specification: males and females (shown separately) in the U. S., 1900; male and females in India, 1961. In many of the tables there has been a considerable amount of even more detailed specification. Therefore, care must be taken to determine, for each table, the exact specifications of the population or populations referred to.

One of the purposes of this collection of tables is to present a statistical picture of American society today. However, in order to provide a basis for evaluating this statistical description, some comparisons with other dates and other places have been included. It was not always possible, or always desirable, to present data for the same places and the same dates in each table.

To summarize what has been said up to now: First, read carefully the title of the table, noting the nature of the table and the population referred to. Next, examine the specific categories in terms of which the data are presented, including whatever footnotes may be provided in connection with them. Then, study the organization of the categories. Finally, examine the numbers and try to grasp their significance. One must also find out whether the figures are presented in terms of thosuands or millions. A count of 50,215,425 may appear as 50.2, with the 000,000's indicated in the headings.

It is not appropriate here to try to present all the varieties and complexities of tabular organization, but perhaps a discussion of two major aspects of organization will illustrate the scope of the matter. (For a more complete and systematic discussion of the subject, see Hans Zeisel, *Say It With Figures*, 4th edition, Harper and Bros., New York, 1957, chapters 1, 2 and 4. While referring to other sources, it is worth calling attention to the valuable instruction on how to analyze statistical tables contained in W. Allen Wallis and Harry V. Roberts, *Statistics: A New Approach*, The Free Press, Glencoe, Ill., 1956, pp. 270-279.)

Some tables aim at making clear differences between certain categories at a particular time. Other tables aim at showing change over time. Sometimes these two aims are combined. For example, the social correlates of non-voting (Table 3.41) are presented in terms of the differences between categories such as men and women, younger and older, and white and Negro with respect to the percentage that did not vote. (Although these differences are shown for two dates, this has been done only to provide a basis for deciding whether the differences are a relatively constant feature of political behavior. This, it might be argued, is *some* sort of trend analysis, but it is, in any case, distinct from examining whether or not the *size* of the differences has been changing over time.) A time series is found in the data relative to the extension of the franchise (Table 3.40), indicating the changes in the proportion of the total population that was eligible to vote in presidential elections from 1860 to 1960. Finally, a table showing the growth of selected health professions (Table 4.54) presents data showing the increase in the U. S. in the number of doctors, dentists, and nurses between 1900 and 1960. In this table, the aim is to show not only the trend in each professional category, but also the differences in the rates of increase between them.

These examples refer to the United States and to the United States only. As noted above, there are also tables comparing the United States with other countries. All but two of these tables show a comparison at (approximately) a single point in time. (See, for example, the comparison of the crude marriage and divorce rates around 1955 in Table 1.64). Of the remaining two, one compares countries with respect to the changing age distribution (Table 1.31) and the other compares the rates of social mobility (Table 4.55).

Speaking very generally, we may say that there are only two kinds of figures in a table, basic and derived. Basic data are obtained by counting; derived data are obtained by computing averages, ratios, indices, or percentages from data based on a count. For example, in the table showing "extensions of the franchise" and "changes in participation in presidential elections" (Table 3.40), one column of basic data and two columns of derived data are presented. The basic data are the counts of the total population for each of the election years shown. The derived data are percentages: the percentage of the total population that was eligible to vote for each election year shown, and the percentage of eligible voters who actually voted. From these percentages and the count of the total population, it is possible to derive, if necessary, the two counts which are not shown in the table, namely, the count of the number of eligibles and of the number of voters. Thus, the table contains all the necessary information, in a form which makes its point clearer than if only basic data were used. Furthermore, its point is made more simply than if both basic and derived data were included. Clarity and simplicity are gained by sacrificing completeness.

In general, the more derived data it seems desirable to include in a table (for the sake of clarity or simplicity or comprehensiveness), the more necessary it becomes to compromise on completeness, that is, to omit basic data. A good example is the table showing changes in school enrollment, by age (Table 5.50). In order to be able to present six age groups for each of three dates in a clear and simple way, it was necessary to limit the kind of data to be included in the table. The solution was to omit all basic data and use only percentages. A further economy was to include only the percentage that was enrolled, implying that the remaining percentage was *not enrolled.* For example, the table shows that 63.7 per cent of those 5 and 6 years old were enrolled in 1960, and this, of course, implies that 26.3 per cent of those in this age group were *not* enrolled. Since this is a device frequently but not uniformly used, one should note whether or not the percentages shown in a table are supposed to add up to 100 per cent.

As has been indicated, some tables contain only basic data; others only derived data; and some contain both basic and derived data. The headings tell the reader which numbers are counts and which are ratios, averages, or percentages. Thus, we return again to our basic advice: when you read a statistical table, look at the words first and then at the figures.

M.G.

Tables About American Society

EDITED BY
MURRAY GENDELL

Table 1.10

ESTIMATES OF WORLD POPULATION BY CONTINENTS
1650 - 1975

Millions of Persons

	1650	*1750*	*1850*	*1950*	*1975*[5]
World	**470**	**694**	**1,094**	**2,497**	**3,828**
Africa	100	100	100	199	303
America:	8	11	59	331	543
North[1]	(1)	(1)	(26)	(168)	(240)
Latin[2]	(7)	(10)	(33)	(163)	(303)
Asia[3]	257	437	656	1,380	2,210
Europe[4]	103	144	274	574	751
Oceania	2	2	2	13	21

1. America north of Mexico.
2. America south of the United States.
3. Excluding the Asiatic part of the U.S.S.R.
4. Including the Asiatic part of the U.S.S.R.
5. "Medium" expectation.

Source: For 1650-1850, United Nations, *Proceedings of the World Population Conference, 1954,* vol. 3, New York, 1955, "The Past and Future Population of the World and Its Continents," table 1, p. 266. For 1950 and 1975, United Nations, *The Future Growth of World Population,* New York, 1958, table 5, p. 23.

Table 1.11

AREA AND POPULATION OF THE UNITED STATES
1790 - 1960

	Area in Square Miles (in 000's)[1]		*Population*		*Increase over Preceding Decade*	
Year	*Land*	*Water*	*Number (in 000,000's)*	*Per Square Mile of Land Area*	*Number (in 000,000's)*	*Per Cent*
1790	865	24	3.9	4.5	—	—
1850	2,940	53	23.2	7.9	6.1	35.9
1900	2,970	53	76.0	25.6	13.0	20.7
1930	2,977	45	122.8	41.2	17.0	16.1
1940	2,977	45	131.7	44.2	8.9	7.2
1950	2,975	48	150.7	50.7	19.0	14.5
1960[2]	3,549	66	179.3	50.5	28.6	19.0

1. Area figures for each census year represent all continental areas under jurisdiction of U. S. on indicated date, including in some cases considerable areas not then organized or settled and not covered by the census. Area figures have been adjusted to bring them into agreement with remeasurements made in 1940.
2. Includes Alaska and Hawaii. Without them, population was 178.5 million.

Source: U. S. Bureau of the Census, *Statistical Abstract of the United States: 1962,* Washington, D.C., 1962, table 1, p. 5.

Table 1.12

POPULATION OF THE UNITED STATES, BY REGIONS, AND PER CENT INCREASE, 1790 - 1960

Population (000's)	*Northeast*	*North Central*	*South*	*West*	**U.S.**
1790	1,968	—	1,961	—	**3,929**
1850	8,627	5,404	8,983	179	**23,192**
1900	21,047	26,333	24,524	4,091	**75,995**
1960	44,678	51,619	54,973	28,053	**179,323**
Per Cent Increase	*%*	*%*	*%*	*%*	*%*
1790-1850	338	—	358	—	**490**
1850-1900	144	387	173	2,185	**228**
1900-1960	112	96	124	586	**137**

Source: For 1790-1900, U. S. Bureau of Census, *Historical Statistics of the United States, Colonial Times to 1957*, Washington, D. C., 1960, Series A95-122, pp. 11-12. For 1960, U. S. Bureau of the Census. *U. S. Census of Population: 1960. General Population Characteristics, U. S. Summary.* Final Report PC(1)-1B (Washington, D. C.: Government Printing Office, 1961), table 52, p. 159.

Table 1.20

INCREASE IN POPULATION, NET ARRIVALS, AND NATURAL INCREASE IN THE UNITED STATES IN SELECTED DECADES, 1820 - 1960

Decade	*Total Increase*[1] *(000's)*	*Natural Increase*[1] *(000's)*	*Net Arrivals*[1] *(000's)*
1820-1830	3,228	3,105	123
1840-1850	6,122	4,702	1,420
1860-1870	8,375	6,291	2,102
1880-1890	12,792	7,527	4,966
1900-1910	15,978	9,656	6,294
1920-1930	17,064	14,500	3,187
1940-1950	19,028	17,666	1,362
1950-1960[2]	28,290	25,310	2,980

1. Total increase, as reported by the U. S. Bureau of the Census. Natural increase and net arrivals are estimated. For nature of estimates, see source, table 91, p. 294. The figures for many of the decades do not balance because net arrivals and natural increase could only be approximated.
2. Includes Alaska and Hawaii.

Source: Conrad Taeuber and Irene B. Taeuber, *The Changing Population of the United States*, John Wiley and Sons, New York, 1958, table 91, p. 294, for all data except those for 1950-1960. They are from, U. S. Bureau of the Census, *Current Population Reports,* Series P. 25, No. 250 (July 3, 1962).

Table 1.21

CRUDE BIRTH AND DEATH RATES,[1] AND RATE OF NATURAL INCREASE, FOR SELECTED COUNTRIES, 1960[2]

	Birth Rates	*Death Rates*	*Rates of Natural Increase*[3]
United States	23.6*	9.5*	14.1*
Sweden	13.7	10.0	3.7
Japan	17.2*	7.6*	9.6*
Soviet Union	24.9	7.1	17.8
Puerto Rico	31.7*	6.7*	25.0*
Taiwan	39.5	6.9	32.6
Tunisia	43.7	10.8	32.9
Mexico	45.0	11.4	33.6

* Provisional.

1. Crude rates indicate the number of births or deaths for every 1,000 persons of all ages.
2. The selection of countries has been limited by the fact that many countries do not yet have reliable vital statistics.
3. The rate of natural increase is merely the difference between the birth rate and the death rate.

Source: United Nations, *Demographic Yearbook 1961* (New York, 1961), table 6, pp. 162ff., for birth rates and table 14, pp. 264ff., for the death rates. Rates of natural increase obtained by calculation.

Table 1.22

PROJECTION TO 1980 OF THE POPULATION OF THE UNITED STATES, BY AGE[1]

	Persons (000's)		
	1960 (Actual)	*1980 (Projected)*	*Per Cent Increase*
All ages	**179.324**	**259,584**	**45**
Under 5	20,321	32,505	59
5 - 9	18,692	28,762	54
10 - 14	16,773	25,223	50
15 - 19	13,219	22,312	69
20 - 24	10,801	20,507	90
25 - 29	10,869	19,087	75
30 - 44	36,031	42,529	18
45 - 64	36,058	44,201	23
65 and over	16,560	24,458	48

1. The fertility assumption in this projection is that the gross reproduction rate (1.79) for the period 1955-57 (about the same as the 1958-60 level) will remain constant until 1980. For other (higher and lower) fertility assumptions—there were three others—see the source. Further, it was assumed in all the projections that the level of mortality will continue to decline gradually and that net immigration will average 300,000 per year, approximately equal to the average during 1951-56.

Source: U. S. Bureau of the Census, *Current Population Reports,* Series P-25, No. 251. (July 6, 1962), p. 4.

Table 1.30

AGE AND SEX COMPOSITION OF THE POPULATION OF THE UNITED STATES, 1900 AND 1960

	Per Cent Distribution		*Males per 1,000 Females*	
Age	*1900*	*1960*	*1900*	*1960*
Under 15 years	34.5	31.1	1021	1034
15 - 24	19.6	13.4	981	1013
25 - 44	28.1	26.1	1088	969
45 - 64	13.7	20.1	1107	958
65 and over	4.1	9.2	1020	828
All	**100.0**	**100.0**	**1041**	**978**
Median Age	22.9	29.5		

Sources: For age in 1900, *Historical Statistics of the U. S., op. cit.*, Series A71-85, p. 10; in 1960, *U. S. Census of Population: 1960*. Final Report PC(1)-1B, *op. cit.*, table 47, p. 153. For sex ratio, in 1900, U. S. Bureau of the Census, *Statistical Abstract of the United States: 1960*, Washington, D. C., 1960, table 17, p. 22; in 1960, *Statistical Abstract of the United States: 1962, op. cit.*, table 16, p. 24.

Table 1.31

AGE DISTRIBUTION OF THE UNITED STATES AND SELECTED FOREIGN COUNTRIES, 1880 AND 1960 (OR APPROXIMATE DATES)

		Per Cent Distribution		
U.S.	*Under 20*	*20-64*	*65 and over*	**Total**
1960	38.5	52.2	9.2	**100.0**
1880	48.1	48.5	3.4	**100.0**
France				
1960	31.8	56.2	12.0	**100.0**
1881	35.4	56.5	8.1	**100.0**
India				
1961	49.3	45.3[1]	5.4[2]	**100.0**
1881	46.9	47.8[1]	5.3[2]	**100.0**
Soviet Union				
1959	37.5	53.1[1]	9.4[2]	**100.0**
1897	48.6	44.5[1]	6.9[2]	**100.0**

1. Age 20-59.
2. Age 60 and over.

Source: For the 19th century data, Warren S. Thompson, *Population Problems*, 4th ed., McGraw-Hill, New York, 1953, table 6-2, p. 95. The 1959 and 1960 data are taken from the *Demographic Yearbook 1961*, table 5, pp. 146-147 and 160-161. The data for India, 1961 are from V.R.K. Tilak, "The Future Manpower Situation in India, 1961-76," *International Labour Review*, Vol`87, No. 5 (May, 1963), table 2, p. 437.

Table 1.40

COLOR AND NATIVITY COMPOSITION OF THE POPULATION OF THE UNITED STATES AND ITS REGIONS, 1900 AND 1960

		Per Cent Distribution in			
1900	**U.S.**	*Northeast*	*North Central*	*South*	*West*
White	**87.9**	98.0	97.9	67.4	94.6
Native	**74.5**	75.5	82.1	65.1	76.0
Foreign-born	**13.4**	22.5	15.8	2.3	18.6
Non-White	**12.1**	2.0	2.1	32.6	5.3
Negro	**11.6**	1.9	1.9	32.3	0.7
Other	**0.5**	0.1	0.2	0.3	4.6
Total	**100.0**	100.0	100.0	100.0	100.0
1960					
White	**88.6**	92.9	93.0	79.1	92.1
Native	**83.4**	83.0	88.7	77.4	86.0
Foreign-born	**5.2**	9.9	4.3	1.7	6.1
Non-White	**11.4**	7.1	7.0	20.9	8.0
Negro	**10.5**	6.8	6.7	20.6	3.9
Other	**0.9**	0.3	0.3	0.3	4.1
Total	**100.0**	100.0	100.0	100.0	100.0

Source: 1900: *Historical Statistics of the United States, op. cit.,* Series A95-122, pp. 11-12. For 1960, U. S. Bureau of the Census, *U. S. Census of Population: 1960. Detailed Characteristics. United States Summary.* Final Report PC(1)-1D Washington, D.C., 1963, table 233, pp. 615-618.

Table 1.41

EXPECTATION OF LIFE AT BIRTH, BY COLOR AND SEX, IN THE UNITED STATES, 1900, 1933, AND 1959[1]

	1900[2]	*1933*	*1959*
Total			
Both sexes	**47.3**	**63.3**	**69.7**
Male	64.3	61.7	66.5
Female	48.3	65.1	73.0
White			
Both sexes	47.6	64.3	70.5
Male	46.6	62.7	67.3
Female	48.7	66.3	73.9
Non-White			
Both sexes	33.0	54.7	63.5
Male	32.5	53.5	60.9
Female	33.5	56.0	66.2

1. The expectation of life at birth is the average number of years that members of a hypothetical cohort would live if they were subject throughout their lives to the age-specific mortality rates observed at the time of their birth. (Source, pp. 5-1, 5-2).
2. In 1900, only ten states, a number of cities, and the District of Columbia were included in the death-registration area. This represented 40% of the population of the U. S. By 1933, 48 states and D.C. were in the death-registration area. Alaska was added in 1959. (Source, pp. 1-7, 1-8.)

Source: *Vital Statistics of the United States, 1959,* Vol. I, *Introductory Text and General Tables* (Washington, D. C.: Government Printing Office, 1961), table 5-D, p. 5-8.

Table 1.42

CRUDE DEATH RATE, BY COLOR AND SEX, IN THE UNITED STATES, 1900, 1933, AND 1960[1]

	1900	*1933*	*1960*
Total	**17.2**	**10.7**	**9.5**
Male	17.9	11.6	10.9
Female	16.5	9.7	8.0
White			
Both sexes	17.0	10.3	9.4
Male	17.7	11.2	10.9
Female	16.3	9.3	8.0
Non-White			
Both sexes	25.0	14.1	10.0
Male	25.7	15.1	11.4
Female	24.4	13.1	8.6

1. Number of deaths, excluding fetal deaths, per 1,000 population. Prior to 1933 only for areas included in the national death-registration statistics.

Source: For 1900 and 1933, *ibid.*, table 6-A, p. 6-11. For 1960, *Statistical Abstract of the United States: 1962, op. cit.*, table 67, p. 63.

Table 1.50

HOSPITALS, HOSPITAL BEDS, AND PATIENTS IN THE UNITED STATES, 1947 AND 1960

	1947	*1960*
Number of hospitals	6,173	6,876
Number of hospital beds (000's)	1,436	1,658
Ratio: hospital beds/1,000 population[1]	9.7	9.2
Number of patients admitted (000's)	17,789	25,027
Average hospital census (000's)[2]	1,190	1,402

1. Population excludes Armed Forces overseas.
2. Average number of patients receiving hospital treatment each day.

Source: *Ibid.*, table 93, p. 79 and table 94, p. 80.

Table 1.51

AVAILABLE, USED, AND REJECTED MANPOWER IN THE U. S. ARMY, WORLD WAR II

	Millions of Males	
Total Manpower Considered for Service		**22.9**
Deferred	4.4[1]	
Rejected after Examination	5.7[2]	
Separated from Service	2.5[3]	
Total Unusable Manpower		12.6
Casualties	.25	
Surviving Used Manpower	10.0	
Total Usable Manpower		10.3

1. More than 3 million were between 30 and 37 years of age.
2. 66% because of physical defects, 19% because of emotional defects, and 14% because of mental-educational defects.
3. 3% non honorable, 5% inaptitude, 13% physical disability, 22% psychiatric disability, 57% other reasons, usually over-age.

N.B.: Figures are approximate.

Source: Compiled from information in Eli Ginzberg *et al.*, *The Lost Divisions,* Columbia University Press, New York, 1959.

Table 1.60
PER CENT DISTRIBUTION OF THE POPULATION, BY MARITAL STATUS AND BY SEX, IN THE UNITED STATES, 1900 AND 1960

	Male		*Female*	
	1900	*1960*	*1900*	*1960*
Single	42.0	25.1	33.3	19.1
Married	53.0	69.1	55.5	65.9
Widowed	4.5	3.6	10.8	12.2
Divorced	0.4	2.1	0.4	2.8

Source: For 1900, *Historical Statistics of the U. S., op. cit.*, Series A210-227, p. 15; for 1960, *U. S. Census of Population: 1960.* Final Report PC(1)-1B, *op. cit.*, table 61, p. 174.

Table 1.61
PROPORTIONS OF MEN AND WOMEN AGED 45-54 YEARS THAT WERE SINGLE[1] IN SELECTED COUNTRIES, FOR VARIOUS RECENT DATES

		Per Cent	
Country	*Year*	*Men*	*Women*
Ireland	1951	30.9	25.8
Sweden	1950	15.6	19.2
Chile	1951	13.7	16.1
France	1954	10.3	10.4
United States	1950	8.5	7.8
India	1951	3.9	1.2
Japan	1955	1.2	1.5

1. "Single" excludes "married," "widowed," and "divorced."

Source: *United Nations, Demographic Yearbook 1958* (New York, 1958), table 6, pp. 138ff.

Table 1.62
MEDIAN AGE OF HUSBAND AND WIFE AT SELECTED STAGES OF THE LIFE CYCLE OF THE AMERICAN FAMILY, 1890, 1940, 1950, AND 1959

Stage of	*Median Age of Husband*				*Median Age of Wife*			
Family Life Cycle	*1890*	*1940*	*1950*	*1959*	*1890*	*1940*	*1950*	*1959*
First marriage	26.1	24.3	22.8	22.3	22.0	21.5	20.1	20.2
Birth of last child[1]	36.0	29.9	28.8	27.9	31.9	27.1	26.1	25.8
Marriage of last child	59.4	52.8	50.3	49.2	55.3	50.0	47.6	47.1
Death of one spouse[2]	57.4	63.6	64.1	65.7[4]	53.3	60.9	61.4	63.6[4]
Death of other spouse[3]	66.4	69.7	71.6		67.7	73.5	77.2	

1. Median age of wife in 1950 at birth of first child was 22.5.
2. Husband and wife survive jointly from marriage to specified age.
3. Husband (wife) survives separately from marriage to specified age.
4. Either spouse.

Source: Paul C. Glick, "The Life Cycle of the Family," *Marriage and Family Living*, vol. 17 (1955), table 1, p. 4. Figures for 1959 updated by Dr. Glick for use in Marvin S. Sussman (editor), *Sourcebook in Marriage and the Family*, Houghton Mifflin Co., Boston, 1963.

Table 1.63

MARRIAGE AND DIVORCE RATES IN THE UNITED STATES, SELECTED DATES, 1920-1959

	Marriage Rates		*Divorce Rates*	
	Per 1,000 Population	*Per 1,000 Unmarried Females*[1]	*Per 1,000 Population*	*Per 1,000 Unmarried Females*[1]
1920	12.0	92.0	1.6	8.0
1930	9.2	67.6	1.6	7.5
1932[2]	7.9	56.0	1.3	6.1
1940	12.1	82.8	2.0	8.8
1945	12.2	83.6	3.5	14.4
1946[2]	16.4	118.1	4.3	17.9
1947	13.9	106.2	3.4	13.6
1950	11.1	90.2	2.6	10.3
1955	9.3	80.9	2.3	9.3
1959	8.5	73.6	2.2	9.3

1. Fifteen years of age and over.
2. 1932 was the low point and 1946 the peak.

Source: *Vital Statistics of the United States: 1959*, vol. I, *op. cit.*, tables 2-A and 2-B, p. 2-17.

Table 1.64

NUMBER OF MARRIAGES AND DIVORCES PER 1,000 POPULATION IN SELECTED COUNTRIES, 1955

	Marriages Contracted	*Divorce Decrees*
United States	9.3	2.3
Egypt	9.1	2.4
Israel[1]	8.7	1.2 (1956)
Puerto Rico	8.4	2.0
England and Wales	8.1	0.6 (1956)
Japan	8.0	0.8 (1956)
France	7.2	0.7
Sweden	7.2	1.2 (1956)
Ceylon	6.0	0.2
Ireland	5.6	*
Venezuela	5.3	0.2 (1954)

* No legal provision for divorce in the sense used in the source.

1. Jewish population.

Source: *Demographic Yearbook: 1958, op. cit.*, table 16 (marriage) and table 25 (divorce).

Table 1.65

CHILDREN AND DIVORCES IN THE UNITED STATES, 1953-1959

	Number of Divorces (000's)	*Per cent of Divorces with Children Involved*	*Ratio of Children per Divorce*
1953	390	45.5	0.85
1954	379	47.8	0.90
1955	377	48.1	0.92
1956	382	48.9	0.95
1957	381	50.9	1.00
1958	368	59.8	*
1959	395	64.4	*

* Not computed.

Source: *Vital Statistics of the United States: 1959*, vol. I, *op. cit.*, p. 2-14 and table 2-A, p. 2-17.

Table 1.70

NUMBER OF LIVE BIRTHS PER 1,000 WOMEN, BY AGE, IN THE UNITED STATES, SELECTED DATES, 1940-1959[1]

Age	*1940*	*1950*	*1959*
15-44[2]	**79.9**	**106.2**	**120.2**
10-14	0.7	1.0	0.9
15-19	54.1	81.6	90.9
20-24	135.6	196.6	256.4
25-29	122.8	166.1	200.6
30-34	83.4	103.7	116.1
35-39	46.3	52.9	58.5
40-44	15.6	15.1	15.7
45-49[3]	1.9	1.2	1.0

1. Data adjusted for under-registration of births. (1960 data shown in the source are for registered births only.)
2. Rates computed by relating total births, regardless of age of mother, to female population aged 15-44 years.
3. Rates computed by relating births to mothers aged 45 years and over to female population aged 45-49 years.

Source: *Vital Statistics of the United States: 1960,* vol. I—Section 1, *Natality—General Summary* (Washington, D. C.: Government Printing Office, 1962), table 1-E, p. 1-19.

Table 1.71

PER CENT DISTRIBUTION OF HOUSEHOLDS, BY SIZE, IN THE UNITED STATES IN 1790, 1890, AND 1960

Size of Household	*1790*	*1890*	*1960*
1 Person	3.7	3.6	13.1
2 Persons	7.8	13.2	27.8
3 Persons	11.7	16.7	18.9
4 Persons	13.8	16.8	17.6
5 Persons	13.9	15.1	11.5
6 Persons	13.2	11.6	5.7
7 Persons	11.2	8.5	} 5.4
8 Persons	9.0	5.9	
9 Persons	6.5	3.8	
10 or more	9.1	4.8	
All	**100.0**	**100.0**	**100.0**
Median size (in persons)	5.4	4.5	3.0

Source: Paul C. Glick, *American Families,* John Wiley and Sons, New York, 1957, table 14, p. 22, for all but 1960. The latter comes from U. S. Bureau of the Census, *Current Popualtion Reports,* Series P-20, Number 106 (January 9, 1961), table 3, p. 13.

Table 1.72

NUMBER OF CHILDREN EVER BORN PER 1,000 WOMEN EVER MARRIED, BY AGE, IN THE UNITED STATES, 1910, 1940, AND 1959

Age	*1910*	*1940*	*1959*[1]
15-44	**2,866**[1]	**1,904**[1]	**2,304**
45-59	4,744	2,998	2,366
50-54	4,972	3,146	} 2,864
55-59	5,218	3,301	
60-64	5,266	3,462	
65-69	5,364	3,700	
70-74	5,395	3,901	

1. *Statistical Abstract of the U.S. 1960, op. cit.,* table 61, p. 58.

Source: (for everything except data accounted for in footnote 1) *Historical Statistics of the U. S., op. cit.,* Series B69-75, p. 24.

Table 1.73

NUMBER OF CHILDREN EVER BORN AS OF 1957 PER 1,000 WOMEN EVER MARRIED AND HUSBAND PRESENT, BY INCOME OF HUSBAND IN 1956

Husband's Income (1956)	*Women Aged 15-44*	*Women Aged 45 and over*
Under $1,000	2,857	3,829
$1,000 - 2,000	2,671	3,414
$2,000 - 3,000	2,330	3,044
$3,000 - 4,000	2,267	2,794
$4,000 - 5,000	2,232	2,403
$5,000 - 7,000	2,306	2,300
$7,000 and over	2,348	2,134
All	**2,320**	**2,866**

Source: U. S. Bureau of the Census, *Statistical Abstract of the United States: 1962* (Washington, D. C.: Government Printing Office, 1962), table 59, p. 58.

Table 1.74

NUMBER OF CHILDREN EVER BORN PER 1,000 WOMEN EVER MARRIED, BY RELIGION AND BY AGE, IN THE UNITED STATES, 1957

	Women 15-44 Years Old		*Women 45 Years Old and Over*	
	Number of Women (000's)	*Children ever Born per 1,000 Women*	*Number of Women (000's)*	*Children ever Born per 1,000 Women*
Protestant	18,159	2,220	16,550	2,753
Baptist	6,020	2,359	4,224	3,275
Lutheran	1,762	2,013	1,870	2,382
Methodist	3,668	2,155	3,795	2,638
Presbyterian	1,495	2,001	1,445	2,188
Other Protestant	5,214	2,237	5,216	2,702
Roman Catholic	6,999	2,282	5,319	3,056
Jewish	746	1,749	905	2,218
Other, none, and not reported	852	2,069	846	2,674
All	**26,756**	**2,218**	**23,620**	**2,798**

Source: U. S. Bureau of the Census, *Statistical Abstract of the U.S.: 1959,* Washington, D.C., 1959, table 61, p. 57.

Table 1.75

GROSS AND NET REPRODUCTION RATES IN THE UNITED STATES, BY COLOR, SELECTED DATES, 1905 TO 1959

Gross Reproduction Rate[2]	*1905-10*	*1930-35*	*1959*[1]
Total	**1,793**	**1,108**	**1,806**
White	1,740	1,080	1,730
Non-white	2,240	1,336	2,354
Net Reproduction Rate[2]			
Total	**1,336**	**984**	**1,736**
White	1,339	972	1,672
Non-white	1,329	1,074	2,196

1. Based on births adjusted for under-registration.
2. Reproduction rates provide an indication of the extent to which a population is capable of replacing itself through reproduction. Gross rates do not take into account the prevailing mortality rates, whereas net rates do. A net reproduction rate of 1,000 (assuming no change in the rate and ignoring migration) means that the population would replace itself in a generation. Under the same assumptions, if the rate is 2,000, the population would double in a generation; if the rate is 500, the population would be halved.

Source: For 1905-10 and 1930-35, *Historical Statistics of the U. S., op. cit.,* Series B31-36, p. 23; for 1959, *Vital Statistics of the United States 1960,* Vol. I, Section 1, *op. cit.,* table 1-D, p. 1-18.

Table 2.00

SELECTED RESOURCES IN USE IN THE UNITED STATES AND THE SOVIET UNION, 1961

	Millions of short tons			*Per Cent*		
	U.S.	*U.S.S.R.*	*World*	*U.S.*	*U.S.S.R.*	*World*
Wheat production	37.0	7.9	**260.7**	14.2	3.0	**100.0**
Meat consumption	14.3	8.7	**69.6**	20.5	12.5	**100.0**
Energy consumption[1]	1628.8	701.0	**4772.0**	34.1	14.7	**100.0**
Steel production	98.0	77.9	**391.1**	25.1	19.9	**100.0**

[1] In coal equivalents.

Source: United Nations, *Statistical Yearbook 1962,* tables 15, 122, 127, and 132. Recalculated into short tons for use in *Statistical Abstract of the U. S. 1963* by the Bureau of the Census.

Table 3.12

OCCUPATIONAL BACKGROUND OF POLITICAL DECISION-MAKERS IN THE UNITED STATES, VARIOUS DATES

Occupational Class	*President, Vice-Pres., Cabinet*[1] 1877-1934	*United States Senators* 1949-51	*United States Representatives* 1949-51	*State Governors* 1930-40	*State Legislators*[2] 1925-35	*Labor Force* 1940
Professionals	74%	69%	69%	60%	36%	7%
Lawyers	(70)	(57)	(56)	(52)	(28)	—
Others	(4)	(12)	(13)	(8)	(8)	—
Proprietors & officials	21	24	22	25	25	8
Farmers	2	7	4	11	22	11
Low-salaried workers	1	0	1	1	4	17
Wage earners	2	0	2	1	3	40
Servants	0	0	0	0	0	11
Farm Laborers	0	0	0	0	0	7
Unknown, unclassified	0	0	2	3	10	0
All	**100**	**100**	**100**	**101**	**100**	**101**
	(n=176)	(n=109)	(n=435)	(n=170)	(n=12,689)	

1. Occupations in this column are those for which presidents, vice-presidents, and cabinet officers were trained.
2. Figures for the lower houses of 13 selected states and the upper houses of 12. The states are Arkansas, California (lower house only), Illinois, Indiana, Iowa, Louisiana, Maine, Minnesota, Mississippi, New Jersey, New York, Pennsylvania, Washington.

Source: Donald R. Matthews, *The Social Background of Political Decision-Makers,* Random House, Inc., New York, 1954, table 7, p. 30.

Table 3.20
GROWTH OF NON-MILITARY GOVERNMENT EMPLOYMENT IN THE UNITED STATES FOR SELECTED DATES, 1920 TO 1961

Year	*Number of Employees*[1] *(000's)*
1920	2,603
1930	3,149
1940	4,202
1950[2]	6,026
1961[2]	8,831

1. Includes all full-time and part-time employees who worked during, or received pay for, any part of the pay period reported. Excludes the Armed Forces. Includes federal, state and local governments.

2.

	State and local governments	*Federal government*
1950	4,098	1,928
1961	6,549	2,281
Percent increase	60	18

Source: Before 1950, *Statistical Abstract of the U. S. 1959, op. cit.*, tables 269 and 271, pp. 210 and 213; 1950 and 1961, *Statistical Abstract of the U. S. 1962, op. cit.*, table 291, p. 222.

Table 3.21
MILITARY PERSONNEL ON ACTIVE DUTY, BY BRANCH OF SERVICE AND RANK, IN THE UNITED STATES, JUNE 30, 1961[1]

Branch and Rank	*Number (000's)*	
Army		
Officers	99.9	
Enlisted	758.7	
Total		858.6
Navy		
Officers	70.0	
Enlisted	557.1	
Total		627.1
Marine Corps		
Officers	16.1	
Enlisted	160.8	
Total		176.9
Air Force		
Officers	128.8	
Enlisted	692.4	
Total		821.2
Coast Guard		
Officers	4.1	
Enlisted	27.5	
Total		31.6
Grand Total		**2,515.4**

1. Includes National Guard, Reserve and retired Regular personnel on extended or continuous active duty. Warrant officers and flight officers included under officers. Military Academy Cadets, Naval Academy Midshipmen, Air Force Academy Cadets, Coast Guard Academy Cadets, and other officer candidates included under enlisted men.

Source: *Statistical Abstract of the U. S. 1962, op. cit.*, tables 337 and 340, pp. 254-255.

Table 3.22

FULL-TIME POLICE DEPARTMENT EMPLOYEES IN THE UNITED STATES, DECEMBER 31, 1961, NUMBER AND RATE PER 1,000 INHABITANTS, BY CITY SIZE

	Number (000's)	*Rate (per 1,000 Inhabitants)*
All Cities[1]	**189.1**	**1.9**
City Population Size		
over 250,000	101.6	2.6
100,000-250,000	18.2	1.7
50,000-100,000	18.4	1.6
25,000- 50,000	16.9	1.5
10,000- 25,000	19.1	1.4
less than 10,000	14.9	1.4

1. Based on reports from 3,430 cities, the total population of which was 97,211,848.

Source: Federal Bureau of Investigation, United States Department of Justice, *Uniform Crime Report for the United States:* 1961 (Washington, D.C.: Government Printing Office, 1962, table 33, p. 108.

Table 3.30

NUMBER AND PERCENTAGE OF ARRESTS, BY AGE, SEX, AND RACE, IN THE UNITED STATES, 1961

	Number (000's)	*Per cent (of total)*
Total[1]	**3,851.8**	**100.0**
Age[1]		
Under 18	566.7	14.7
Under 21	892.2	23.2
Under 25	1,270.1	33.0
Sex[1]		
Male	3,417.9	88.7
Female	434.0	11.3
Race[2]		
White	2,424.6	67.1
Negro	1,073.5	30.0
Indian	79.7	2.2
Chinese	1.7	*
Japanese	3.4	0.1
All others	25.3	0.7

* Less than 0.05%.

1. Based on reports from 2,776 cities with a population exceeding 2,500, the total population of which was 85,158,360.
2. The total number of arrests shown in source is 3,608,317; based on reports from 2,759 cities over 2,500, the total population of which was 75,553,307.

Source: *Uniform Crime Report: 1961, op. cit.*, tables 21-23, pp. 95-97.

Table 3.31

INDEX OF CRIME, BY AREA, UNITED STATES, 1961

	United States		*Rate per 100,000 People*		
	No. of Offenses	*Rate per 100,000*	*SMSA*[1]	*Other Cities*[2]	*Rural*[3]
All offenses	**1,926,119**	**1,052.8**	**1,332.4**	**719.3**	**459.6**
Murder and non-negligent manslaughter	8,599	4.7	4.5	3.6	5.9
Forcible rape	16,012	8.8	10.4	4.1	6.8
Robbery	91,659	50.1	71.2	14.2	11.5
Aggravated assault	133,020	72.7	88.6	47.1	42.7
Burglary	852,506	466.0	570.6	357.0	234.8
Larceny $50 and over	498,117	272.3	345.3	187.7	115.7
Auto theft	326,206	178.3	241.7	105.5	42.1

1. Standard Metropolitan Statistical Areas. These rates are estimated from reports from 98.3% of all SMSA's.
2. Area actually reporting: 90.7%.
3. Area actually reporting: 82.5%.

Note: Through a crime index consisting of seven selected offenses, an attempt is made to measure the extent, fluctuation, and distribution of serious crime in the United States. This count is based on these seven offenses being reported to the police or coming directly to their attention.

During the calendar year 1961 crime reports were received from 7,800 law enforcement agencies representing 96 per cent of the total United States population.

Presentation of crime data by areas follows as closely as practical the definitions used by the Bureaus of the Budget and Census.

The uniformity of the data collected is a prime concern of the Federal Bureau of Investigation, which acts as the national clearing house. The Bureau does more to this end than issue instructions. It also examines each report for arithmetical accuracy and for reasonableness as a possible indication of errors. Furthermore, crime trends for individual places are analyzed by the Bureau five times a year. Any significant increase or decrease is made the subject of a special inquiry with the contributing agency.

For definitions of offenses, see source, pp. 29-30.

Source: *Uniform Crime Reports op. cit.*, table 1, p. 33 and text, pp. 24-31.

Table 3.40

EXTENSIONS OF THE FRANCHISE AND CHANGES IN PARTICIPATION IN PRESIDENTIAL ELECTIONS IN THE UNITED STATES FOR SELECTED DATES, 1860 - 1960

Year	*Population (000,000's)*	*Per cent of Population that was Eligible to Vote*[1]	*Per cent of Eligible Population that Voted*
1860	27.6[2]	17	84
1880	50.3	23	78
1900	76.1	25	74
1920[3]	106.5	51	49
1940	132.0	61	62
1952	157.0	62	64
1956[4]	168.9	61	60
1960[4]	180.7	60	64

1. Eligible population:
   1860—"probably" is an estimate of the population aged 21 and over, minus slaves and those disfranchised by property and citizenship qualifications.
   1880 and 1900—"presumably" refers to all male citizens and all female citizens twenty-one or over in states where they were eligible to vote.
   1940 - 1956—All citizens over the age of 21.
2. Does not include slaves.
3. Prior to 1920, adult women had the right to vote in only a few states. After 1920, adult women had the right to vote throughout the U. S. The fact that 1920 was the first presidential election in which adult women had the right to vote nationally is probably the main reason for the fact that it was the presidential elections of 1920 and 1924 that the smallest percentage of eligibles voted in the history of presidential elections (at least, as shown by the data from 1856):

1912	60%	1924	49%
1916	64%	1928	57%
1920	49%	1932	58%

4. Population counts as of July 1. (The official census date is April 1.)

Source: Robert Lane, *Political Life*, The Free Press, Glencoe, Illinois, 1959, tables 2.1 and 2.2, pp. 19, 21, and 22, for all data except those for 1956 and 1960. For the latter, *Statistical Abstract of the U. S. 1962, op. cit.*, table 2, p. 5 and table 497, p. 373.

Table 3.41

Table 3.41

RELATION OF DEMOGRAPHIC CHARACTERISTICS TO PRESIDENTIAL PREFERENCE AND NON-VOTING IN THE 1948 AND 1952 ELECTIONS IN THE UNITED STATES

Demographic Characteristics	*Per Cent Voted For:* Republican	Democratic	Other[1]	*Per Cent:* Voting	Not Voting	*No. of Cases*[2]
Sex						
1952						
Male	44	34	1	79	21	738
Female	41	28	*	69	31	876
1948						
Male	28	36	5	69	31	302
Female	26	29	4	59	41	357
Age						
1952						
21-34	37	31	*	68	32	485
35-44	41	34	1	76	24	381
45-54	45	33	1	79	21	284
55 and over	48	27	2	77	23	442
1948						
21-34	19	32	5	56	44	199
35-44	24	38	4	66	34	174
45-54	37	33	5	75	25	125
55 and over	31	27	5	63	37	156
Religion						
1952						
Protestant	45	26	1	72	28	1,156
Catholic	41	43	1	85	15	343
1948						
Protestant	28	25	5	58	42	461
Catholic	25	49	5	79	21	140
Race						
1952						
White	47	31	1	79	21	1,453
Negro	6	26	1	33	67	157
1948						
White	29	33	4	66	34	585
Negro	10	18	8	36	64	61
Type of Community						
1952						
Metropolitan areas	44	33	2	79	21	438
Towns and cities	42	31	*	73	27	928
Rural areas	42	25	1	68	32	248
1948						
Metropolitan areas	32	46	5	83	17	182
Towns and cities	30	28	5	63	37	354
Rural areas	12	25	4	41	59	126

Table 3.41 (Continued)

Demographic Characteristics	*Per Cent Voted For:* Republican	Democratic	Other[1]	*Per Cent:* Voting	Not Voting	*No. of Cases*[2]
Education						
1952						
Grade school	31	30	1	62	38	660
High School	46	34	*	80	20	712
College	65	24	1	90	10	238
1948						
Grade school	16	35	4	55	45	292
High school	29	34	4	67	33	266
College	54	17	8	79	21	100
Occupation of Head of Family						
1952						
Prof. & managerial	59	27	2	88	12	333
Other white collar	52	28	1	81	19	155
Skilled & semi-skilled	34	39	1	74	26	462
Unskilled	19	40	1	60	40	174
Farm operators	42	24	1	67	33	178
1948						
Prof. & managerial	58	14	3	75	25	118
Other white collar	38	38	5	81	19	78
Skilled and Semi-skilled	15	52	4	71	29	194
Unskilled	12	33	5	50	50	85
Farm operators	13	25	4	42	58	105
Trade Union Affiliation of Head of Family						
1952						
Member	33	43	1	77	23	411
Non-member	46	26	1	73	27	1,165
1948						
Member	13	55	5	73	27	150
Non-member	32	26	4	62	38	493
Income						
1952						
Under $2,000	30	23	*	53	47	315
$2,000 - 2,999	36	31	1	68	32	255
$3,000 - 3,999	40	35	1	76	24	364
$4,000 - 4,999	41	41	1	83	17	233
$5,000 and over	59	28	1	88	12	415
1948						
Under $2,000	16	28	2	46	54	178
$2,000 - 2,999	17	38	6	61	39	185
$3,000 - 3,999	35	34	5	74	26	142
$4,000 - 4,999	36	33	6	75	25	66
$5,000 and over	53	25	4	82	18	84

* Less than 0.5%.

1. Includes respondents whose vote was not ascertained as well as those who voted for minor-party candidates.
2. The 1952 sample consisted of 1,614 cases; the 1948 sample of 662 cases. The number of cases within a set of demographic groups does not always add to the full total because of the omission of those respondents who did not fall into the categories represented or from whom the relevant information was not obtained.

Source: Angus Campbell, Gerald Gurin and Warren E. Miller, *The Voter Decides,* Row, Peterson and Co., Evanston, 1954, table 5.1, pp. 70-73.

Table 3.50

NUMBER OF NATIONAL ASSOCIATIONS, BY TYPE, IN THE UNITED STATES, 1959[1]

Type	Number
Chambers of commerce[2]	2,693
Trade and commerce	2,314
Education and cultural	563
Health and medical	436
Agricultural organizations and commodity exchanges	327
Social, professional and honorary Greek letter societies	307
Scientific and technical	293
Religious	293
Social welfare	241
Labor unions	224
Nationality and ethnic	212
Public administration, military and legal groups	163
Athletic	123
Fraternal	118
Public affairs	117
Veterans and patriotic	108
Hobby and avocational	98
Horticultural	86
Total	**8,716**

1. The favorite locations of the headquarters of these associations are New York (1,921), Washington, D. C. (869), Chicago (609), and Philadelphia (250).
2. International, bi-national, national, state and local.

Source: Gale Research Co., Detroit, Mich., publishers of the *Encyclopedia of American Associations*.

Table 3.51

MEMBERSHIP IN VOLUNTARY ASSOCIATIONS IN THE UNITED STATES, 1954 AND 1955[1]

Per cent of all Americans belonging to:	*AIPO*[1]	*NORC*[1]
No associations	45%	64%
1 association	30	20
2 associations	16	9
3 associations or more	9	7
Total	**100**	**100**
Sample size	(2,000)	(2,379)

1. Data based on two national surveys, one made by the American Institute of Public Opinion in 1954 and the other by the National Opinion Research Center in 1955. The source argues that AIPO's figures are probably too high and that NORC's are probably too low. Thus, the "true" figures probably lie somewhere in between.

Source: Murray Hausknecht, *The Joiners: A Sociological Description of Voluntary Association Membership in the United States* (New York: Bedminster Press, 1962), table 2:1, p. 23.

Table 3.52

MEMBERSHIP IN VOLUNTARY ASSOCIATIONS IN THE UNITED STATES, BY VARIOUS SOCIAL AND ECONOMIC CHARACTERISTICS, 1954 AND 1955[1]

	Per Cent Belonging to at Least One Voluntary Association	
Home Ownership	*AIPO*[1]	*NORC*[1]
Own residence	*	43
Rent residence	*	25
Education		
Some elementary school	39	17
Elementary school graduate	48	27
Some high school	53	33
High School graduate	64	43
Some college	70	54
College graduate	78	61
Income		
Under $2,000	48	24
$2,000 - 2,999	53	29
$3,000 - 3,999	58	29
$4,000 - 4,999	60	35
$5,000 - 6,999[2]	63	43
$7,000 and over[2]	69	52
Occupation		
Professionals, proprietors, managers, officials	*	53
Clerical and sales	*	41
Skilled labor	*	32
Service	*	27
Semi-skilled labor	*	23
Laborers (except farm)	*	21
Farm owners	*	42
Farm labor		13
Marital Status		
Married	57	38
Widowed	53	30
Divorced and separated	46	27
Single	44	28
Domicile		
City 250,000 and over	47	*
50,000 - 249,000	53	*
10,000 - 49,000	60	*
2,500 - 9,000	68	*
Rural non-farm	56	*
Rural farm	58	*

* Not available.

1. Data based on two national surveys, one made by the American Institute of Public Opinion in 1954 and the other by the National Opinion Research Center in 1955. AIPO's sample size was 2,000 and NORC's was 2,379. The source argues that AIPO's figures are probably too high and that NORC's are probably too low. Thus, the "true" figures probably lie somewhere in between. For the characteristics shown here, however, the *relationship* between them and membership is consistent between the two surveys.
2. For NORC, these income categories are $5,000 - $7,499 and $7,500 and over.

Source: Hausknecht, *op. cit.*, tables 2:2, 2:3, 2:4 and 2:5A, pp. 23-26; table 3:10, pp. 45-46; and table 4:1, p. 57.

Table 3.53

MEMBERSHIP IN NATIONAL AND INTERNATIONAL UNIONS WITH HEADQUARTERS IN THE UNITED STATES FOR SELECTED DATES, 1935 - 1960

	Membership[1] *(000's)*	*Per Cent of*[2] *Total Labor Force*	*Per Cent of*[2] *Employment in Nonagricultural Establishments*
1935	3,728	6.7	13.4
1940	8,944	15.5	27.2
1945	14,796	21.9	35.8
1950	15,000	22.0	31.9
1955	17,749	24.4	33.6
1960	18,117	23.3	32.1

All estimates are based on average number of dues-paying members. Certain unions did not report as members those unemployed, those involved in work stoppages, those in the Armed Forces, apprentices, and retired workers, who were not required to pay dues. Morover, membership in non-interstate independent or unaffiliated unions is excluded.

1. Includes Canadian members of labor unions with headquarters in the United States (1,068,000 in 1960).
2. Percentages calculated on union membership excluding Canadian membership.

Source: *Statistical Abstract of the U. S. 1959, op. cit.*, table 301, p. 238, for 1935 and 1945; *Statistical Abstract of the U. S. 1962, op. cit.*, table 319, p. 241, for other dates.

Table 4.10

DISTRIBUTION OF WORLD POPULATION AND INCOME, 1949

Regions	*Per Cent of World Population*	*Per Cent of World Income*
1. Overseas descendants of Western Europeans[1]	7.5	44.4
United States	(6.5)	(40.9)
2. Western Europe[2]	10.0	21.5
3. U.S.S.R.	8.4	11.2
4. Other Europe[3]	6.4	6.0
5. Latin America[4]	6.6	4.4
6. Asia	52.4	10.5
7. Africa	8.6	2.0
World	**100.0**	**100.0**
Grouping of Regions		
Developed (1 + 2)	17.5	65.9
Semi-developed (3 + 4)	14.8	17.2
Underdeveloped (5 + 6 + 7)	67.6	16.9
World	**100.0**	**100.0**

1. Includes U. S., Canada, Australia, and New Zealand.
2. Includes central and northern Europe, extending through Germany, Czechoslovakia, and Austria in the East.
3. Includes the countries of the Balkan, Appenine, and Iberian peninsulas and the Eastern group.
4. Everything south of the U. S., including the Caribbean.

N. B. "We can get fairly complete coverage of the world for . . . 1949—although only by accepting many suspect statistical estimates. Yet even these rough estimates represent fairly informed and honest judgments backed in part by empirical evidence; and they are useful at least in indicating broad differences or similarities, if not precise magnitudes." (Source, p. 80.)

Source: Simon Kuznets, "Regional Economic Trends and Levels of Living," in Philip M. Hauser (ed.), *Population and World Politics*, The Free Press, Glencoe, Illinois, 1958, table 1, p. 81.

Table 4.11

GROWTH OF GROSS NATIONAL PRODUCT IN THE UNITED STATES FOR SELECTED DATES, 1929 - 1960

	1929	*1940*	*1950*	*1960*	*Per Cent Increase 1929-1960*
Current Dollars					
Total (in billions)	104.4	100.6	284.6	504.4	385
Per capita	857	762	1,876	2,792	225
Constant (1954) dollars					
Total (in billions)	181.8	205.8	318.1	440.8	142
Per capita	1,493	1,558	2,096	2,440	63

Source: *Statistical Abstract of the U.S. 1960, op. cit.*, pp. 304-305 for all dates but 1960. For that date, *Statistical Abstract of the U. S. 1962, op. cit.*, tables 423 and 424, p. 314.

Table 4.20

SUMMARY OF FEDERAL BUDGET RECEIPTS AND EXPENDITURES, 1953 AND 1961

(in millions of dollars)

	1953	*1961*
Receipts		
Individual income taxes	30,108	41,338
Corporation income taxes	21,238	20,954
Excise taxes	9,868	9,063
Employment taxes	274	——
Estate and gift taxes	881	1,896
Customs	596	982
Miscellaneous	1,859	4,080
(Deduct interfund transactions)	(154)	(654)
Total receipts	64,671	77,659
Expenditures		
National defense	50,442	47,494
International affairs and finance	2,216	2,500
Space research and technology	79	744
Agriculture and agricultural resources	2,955	5,173
Natural resources	1,478	2,006
Commerce and transportation	1,926	2,573
Housing and community development	396	320
Health, labor and welfare	2,052	4,244
Education	320	943
Veterans benefits and services	4,368	5,414
Interest	6,578	9,050
General government	1,465	1,709
(Deduct interfund transactions)	(154)	(654)
Total expenditures	**74,120**	**81,515**
Budget surplus (+) or deficit (—)	—9,449	—3,856

Source: *The Budget of the United States Government 1963* (For the fiscal year ending June 30), Washington, D. C., U. S. Government Printing Office, 1962: 1961 table 1, p. 33 and table 11, pp. 49-53; 1953—Receipts: table 12, p. 53; Expenditures: table 14, pp. 110-112.

Table 4.21

FEDERAL BUDGET TOTALS AND PUBLIC DEBT, SELECTED DATES, 1789-1960

(in millions of dollars)

Date	*Receipts*	*Expenditures*	*Surplus (+) or Deficit (—)*	*Public Debt at End of Yr.*
1789-1849	1,160	1,090	+ 70	63
1850-1899	13,895	14,932	— 1,037	1,437
1900	567	521	+ 46	1,263
1910	676	694	— 18	1,147
1920	6,649	6,357	+ 291	24,299
1930	4,058	3,320	+ 738	16,185
1940	5,137	9,055	— 3,918	42,968
1950	36,422	39,544	— 3,122	257,357
1960	77,763	76,539	+ 1,224	286,331

Source: *The Budget of the United States Government 1963, op. cit.*, table 10, p. 42.

Table 4.30

NUMBER AND DISTRIBUTION OF ACTIVE CORPORATIONS, BY SIZE OF ASSETS, IN THE UNITED STATES, 1935 AND 1959

Active Corporations with Assets of:	*1935*		*1959*	
	Number (000's)	*Per Cent*	*Number (000's)*	*Per Cent*
Under $50,000	227.5	54.8	412.1	40.5
$50,000 - $99,999	58.4	14.1	177.5	17.4
$100,000 - $249,999	58.2	14.0	212.6	20.9
$250,000 - $499,999	28.6	6.9	99.6	9.8
$500,000 - $999,999	18.1	4.4	52.0	5.1
$1,000,000 - $4,999,999	18.4	4.4	46.1	4.5
$5,000,000 - $9,999,999	2.8	0.7	8.0	0.8
$10,000,000 - $49,999,999	2.4	0.6	7.5	0.7
$50,000,000 and over	0.7	0.2	2.3	0.2
Total	**415.2**	**100.0**	**1,017.7**	**100.0**

Source: For 1935 *Statistical Abstract of the U. S. 1959, op cit.*, table 620, p. 490; for 1959, *Statistical Abstract of the U. S. 1962, op. cit.*, table 655, p. 493.

Table 4.31

SHARE OF TOTAL ASSETS AND TOTAL NET INCOME OF ACTIVE CORPORATIONS, BY SIZE OF ASSETS, IN THE UNITED STATES, 1959

Active Corporations with Assets of:	*Total Assets (000,000's)*	*Per Cent*	*Net Income (000,000's)*	*Per Cent*
Under $100,000	$ 21,244	1.9	$ 442	0.9
$100,000 - $249,000	$ 33,842	3.0	$ 1,444	3.1
$250,000 - $499,000	$ 34,739	3.1	$ 1.545	3.3
$500,000 - $999,000	$ 36,138	3.2	$ 1,612	3.5
$1,000,000 - $4,999,000	$ 97,228	8.6	$ 4,478	9.6
$5,000,000 - $9,999,000	$ 55,994	4.9	$ 2,222	4.8
$10,000,000- -$49,999,000	$ 154,136	13.6	$ 6,016	12.9
$50,000,000 and over	$ 703,347	61.8	$28,811	61.9
Total	**$1,136,668[1]**	**100.0**	**$46,570**	**100.0**

1. In 1935 total corporation assets were $303,150,000,000.
Source: *Statistical Abstract of the U. S. 1962, op. cit.*, table 656, p. 494.

Table 4.32

ESTIMATE OF OWNERSHIP OF ALL CORPORATIONS IN THE UNITED STATES, BY CLASS OF OWNER, DECEMBER 31, 1957

Class of Owner	*Stockholdings Values in $ Billions*	*Per Cent*
All classes	**$283.0**	**100**
Domestic individuals, adjusted to exclude personal trust funds and nonprofit organizations[1]	202.2	71
Institutions, adjusted to include personal trust funds and nonprofit organizations[1]	74.6	27
Foreigners	6.1	2

1. Since current data on stockholdings are unavailable, the estimate of $45.2 billion for personal trusts and nonprofit organizations was arrived at by taking the SEC's estimate for 1954 ($44 billion; see *Survey of Corporate Pension Funds, 1951 - 1954,* p. 18) and determining what percentage it was of the total stocks outstanding. This percentage, 16.3, was then applied to the total stock value figure for 1957 to yield the estimate of $45.2 billion. The total stock value figure for 1957 includes preferred stocks, while the estimate of $44 billion referred only to common stocks. Thus our estimate for common stocks of personal trust funds and nonprofit organizations could be slightly higher. There are also indications that nonprofit institutions are increasing the percentage of their portfolios invested in common stocks.

Source: Data provided by Securities and Exchange Commission, October 8, 1958, in Paul P. Harbrecht, *Pension Funds and Economic Power,* The Twentieth Century Fund, New York, 1959, table 6, p. 28.

Table 4.33

GROWTH OF STOCK OWNERSHIP IN THE U. S., 1952-1962[1]

	Number of Owners (in millions)	*Approximate Proportion of American Adults*[2]	*Average No. of Shares per Owner*
1952	6.5	1/16	4.10
1956	8.6	1/12	4.25
1959	12.5	1/8	3.50
1962	17.0	1/6	3.40

[1] Data obtained through censuses taken by the N. Y. Stock Exchange; no details as to how censuses were taken.

[2] Age in years not specified.

Source: *The Exchange* [published by the N. Y. Stock Exchange], vol. XXIII, no. 7 (July 1962), p. 1, and the *New York Times*, June 26, 1962, p. 41.

Table 4.40

NUMBER OF FOUNDATIONS FORMED IN THE UNITED STATES, 1900 - 1959[1]

Period	*Number Formed*	*Per Cent*
Before 1900	18	*
1900 - 1909	18	*
1910 - 1919	76	2
1920 - 1929	173	3
1930 - 1939	288	6
1940 - 1949	1,638	32
1950 - 1959	1,839	56
All	**5,550**	**100**

* Less than .5 per cent

1. A foundation is defined as "a nongovernmental, nonprofit organization having a principal fund of its own, managed by its own trustees or directors, and established to maintain or aid social, educational, charitable, religious or other activities serving the common welfare."

Source: The Foundation Library Center, Ann D. Walton and Marianna O. Lewis, editors, *The Foundation Directory*, Edition 2, Russell Sage Foundation, New York, 1964, table 2, p. 13.

Table 4.41

DISTRIBUTION OF GRANTS BY FOUNDATIONS IN THE UNITED STATES, 1959

Field	*Millions of $ granted*	*Per Cent*
Education	315	40
International Activities	106	14
Welfare	96	12
Health	90	12
Sciences	86	11
Religion	46	6
Humanities	40	5
All	**779**	**100**

Source: The Foundation Library Center, *op. cit.*, table 20, p. 44.

Table 4.42

PUBLIC AND PRIVATE EXPENDITURES FOR HEALTH AND MEDICAL CARE, 1928-29 AND 1958-59

Millions of dollars	*Total Expenditures*[1]	*Private Expenditures*	*Public Expenditures*
1928-29	$ 3,625.0	$ 3,112.0	$ 513.0
1958-59	25,195.9[2]	18,965.0	6,230.9
Per Cent			
1928-29	100.0	85.8	14.1
1958-59	100.0	75.3	24.7

1. As per cent of Gross National Product:
   1928-29 3.6
   1958-59 5.4

2. Of this amount, 19.1% went for insurance benefits and costs. In 1949-50, the earliest date shown in the source for which this information is shown separately, only 9.3% went for insurance benefits and costs.

Source: Herman M. Somers and Anne R. Somers, *Doctors, Patients and Health Insurance: The Organization and Financing of Medical Care,* Washington, D.C.: The Brookings Institution, 1961; abridged edition (Garden City, New York: Doubleday and Co., Anchor Books, 1962), table A-1, pp. 508-509.

Table 4.50

NUMBER OF PEOPLE AGED 14 OR MORE IN THE POPULATION AND IN THE LABOR FORCE, BY SEX, 1890 AND 1940-1960

(in millions)

	1890	*1940*	*1950*	*1960*	*Per Cent Increase 1890-1960*	*Per Cent Increase 1940-60*
Male						
Population	21.5	50.8	55.6	61.3	185	21
Labor Force	18.1	40.1	43.8	47.5	162	19
Female						
Population	20.3	50.7	57.2	65.0	220	27
Labor Force	3.7	12.9	16.6	22.4	505	74
Both Sexes						
Population	41.8	101.5	112.8	126.3	203	24
Labor Force	21.8	53.0	60.3	69.9	210	32

Source: number for 1890, Gertrude Bancroft, *The American Labor Force,* (New York: John Wiley and Sons, 1958), table 16, p. 24; number for 1940-1960, U. S. Bureau of the Census. *U. S. Census of Population: 1960. General Social and Economic Characteristics, United States Summary.* Final Report PC(1)–1C. (Washington, D.C.: Government Printing Office, 1962), table 83, p. 214.

Table 4.51

DISTRIBUTION OF WOMEN 14 YEARS OLD AND OVER IN THE LABOR FORCE, BY MARITAL STATUS, IN THE UNITED STATES, 1890, 1950, AND 1960[1]

	Number (000's)			*Per Cent*		
	1890	*1950*	*1960*	*1890*	*1950*	*1960*
All Women	**3,704**	**16,687**	**22,410**	**100.0**	**100.0**	**100.0**
Single	2,566	5,317	5,282	69.3	31.8	23.6
Married	500	8,705	13,610	13.5	52.2	60.7
Widowed or Divorced	638	2,665	3,518	17.2	16.0	15.7

1. These data are based on the decennial censuses. Since 1940 the monthly *Current Population Survey* has provided another source for labor force estimates. In March 1950, the CPS showed 17,795,000 women 14 years old and over in the labor force, of whom 52.1% were married. In March 1961, it showed 24,199,000 women 14 years old and over in the labor force, of whom 60.4% were married. (*Statistical Abstract of the U. S. 1962, op. cit.,* table 294, p. 225.)

   In 1890, 4.5% of all married women 14 years old and over were in the labor force. In March 1961, this percentage was up to 34.0%. (See sources cited.) Of those with (own) children under 6 years of age, however, only 21.1% were in the labor force. (PC(1)-1C, *op cit.,* tables 119 and 120, pp. 265-66.)

Source: Bancroft, *op. cit.,* table 20, p. 35, for 1890 and 1950. For 1960, *U. S. Census of Population: 1960.* Final Report PC(1)–1D, *op. cit.,* table 196, p. 501.

Table 4.52

DISTRIBUTION OF PERSONS ENGAGED IN AGRICULTURE AND NON-AGRICULTURE, AND AS ENTREPRENEURS OR EMPLOYEES, SELECTED YEARS, 1909-1960[1]

	Per Cent			
	1909-13	*1924-28*	*1939-43*	*1958-60*
Total	**100.0**	**100.0**	**100.0**	**100.0**
Agriculture	26.0	20.5	14.0	7.5
Non-agriculture	74.0	79.5	86.0	92.5
Entrepreneurs	*25.0*	*21.5*	*17.5*	*14.0*
Agriculture	15.0	12.0	9.0	4.5
Non-agriculture	10.0	9.5	8.5	9.5
Employees	*75.0*	*78.5*	*82.5*	*86.0*
Agriculture	11.0	8.5	5.0	3.0
Non-agriculture	64.0	70.0	77.5	83.0

1. "The entries are percentages of cumulative totals for the periods shown."
2. Includes, unlike other dates shown, unpaid family workers and those unemployed throughout the year.

Source: Simon Kuznets, "Income Distribution and Changes in Consumption," *The Changing American Population*, Hoke S. Simpson, ed. (New York: Institute of Life Insurance, 1962), table 2, p. 26.

Table 4.53

SHIFTS IN THE OCCUPATIONAL STRUCTURE OF THE UNITED STATES IN 1900, 1950, AND 1960

	Per Cent		
	1900	*1950*[1]	*1960*
Professional, technical and kindred workers	4.2	8.6	11.4
Managers, officials and proprietors (except farm)	5.9	8.8	8.5
Clerical and kindred workers	3.0	12.3	14.9
Sales workers	4.5	7.0	7.4
Craftsmen, foremen and kindred workers	10.6	14.2	14.3
Operatives and kindred workers	12.8	20.3	19.9
Laborers (except farm and mine)	12.4	6.5	5.5
Service workers (except private household)	3.6	7.8	8.9
Private household workers	5.4	2.6	2.8
Farmers and farm managers	19.8	7.5	3.9
Farm laborers and foremen	17.8	4.4	2.4
Total	**100.0**	**100.0**	**100.0**
Number of economically active (000's)[2]	29,030	59,230	67,990

1. These data include adjustments which take account of the differences between the 1950 and 1960 classification systems.
2. The definition of economically active was not the same at each of these dates. For 1900, it refers to all those 10 years old or more who reported a gainful occupation whether or not they were working or seeking work at the time they were interviewed. For 1950 and 1960, it refers to all those 14 years old or more who had previously worked and who were either working for pay or looking for work during a specified week.

Source: For 1900, *Historical Statistics of the U. S., op. cit.*, Series D 72-122, p. 74. For 1950 and 1960, *U. S. Census of Population: 1960*. Final Report PC(1)-1D, *op. cit.*, table 201, pp. 522-527.

Table 4.54

PHYSICIANS, DENTISTS, AND NURSES IN THE UNITED STATES, 1900 AND 1960

	Number (000's)		*Rate: Number per 100,000 Population*	
	1900	*1960*	*1900*	*1960*
Physicians	132.0	256.0	173	142
Dentists	29.7	101.9	39	56
Nurses[1]	50.2[2]	504.0	55[2]	282

1. Active professional graduate nurses.
2. First date for which data are available is 1910.

Source: *Statistical Abstract of the United States: 1962, op. cit.*, table 83, p. 74.

Table 4.55

COMPARATIVE RATES OF UPWARD SOCIAL MOBILITY AMONG MALES WITH FATHERS IN MANUAL OCCUPATIONS[1]

Size of Elite	*Manual into Elite*	*Manual into Non-manual*
A. *Under 4.6%*	%	%
Denmark	1.1	24.1
West Germany	1.5	20.0
India (Poona)	1.4	27.3
B. *6%-8.5%*		
France	3.5	30.1
Great Britain	2.2	24.8
Italy	1.5	8.5
Sweden	3.5	25.5
C. *10%-15%*		
Japan	7.0	23.7
Netherlands	6.6	19.6
Puerto Rico	8.6	14.3
D. *Over 15%*		
Brazil (Sao Paulo)	5.3	29.4
USA	7.8	28.8
USSR (emigrés)	14.5[2]	34.9

1. Based on sample surveys of varying quality taken at various times after World War II. The classification of the occupations of fathers and sons is not done according to exactly the same criteria in the various countries, and the figures should be treated as approximate.
2. This is a figure for the working classes, and therefore overstates manual into the elites.

Source: S. M. Miller, "Comparative Social Mobility" *Current Sociology*, vol. 9, (1960), p. 40.

Table 4.60

LENGTH OF AVERAGE WORK WEEK (IN HOURS) IN AGRICULTURE AND IN NONAGRICULTURAL INDUSTRIES, SELECTED DATES, 1850 - 1960

	All Industries	*Agri-culture*	*Nonagricultural Industries*
1850	69.7	72.0	65.7
1870	65.3	70.0	60.0
1890	61.7	68.0	57.1
1910	54.9	65.0	50.3
1930	45.7	55.0	43.2
1940	43.8	54.6	41.1
1950	39.9	47.2	38.8
1960	38.5	44.0	38.0

Source: Sebastian De Grazia, *Of Time, Work, and Leisure* (New York: The Twentieth Century Fund, 1962), table 1, p. 441.

Table 4.61

PERCENT OF THE CIVILIAN LABOR FORCE UNEMPLOYED, AND AVERAGE DURATION OF UNEMPLOYMENT, 1950-1962*

	Percent	*Average in Weeks*
1950	5.3	12.1
1953	2.9	8.1
1954	5.6	11.7
1955	4.4	13.2
1956	4.2	11.3
1957	4.3	10.4
1958	6.8	13.8
1959	5.5	14.5
1960	5.6	12.8
1961 (whole year)	6.7	15.5
(March)	7.7	15.4
1962 (March)	6.2	16.5

* Annual figures are averages of monthly figures.

Source: *Statistical Abstract of the U. S. 1962, op. cit.*, table 284, p. 217.

Table 4.62

CHARACTERISTICS OF THE UNEMPLOYED, UNITED STATES, 1962

		Per cent Unemployed
Total		**5.6**
Males		**5.3**
(Age)	14-19	13.3
	20-24	8.9
	25-34	4.5
	35-44	3.6
	45-54	3.9
	55-64	4.6
	65 and over	4.6
Females		**6.2**
(Age)	14-19	13.2
	20-24	9-1
	25-34	6.5
	35-44	5.2
	45-54	4.1
	55-64	3.5
	65 and over	4.1
White		4.9
Nonwhite		11.0

	Per Cent Unemployed
Professional, technical and kindred workers	1.7
Managers, officials and non-farm proprietors	1.5
Clerical workers	3.9
Sales workers	4.1
Craftsmen and foremen	5.1
Operatives	7.5
Private household workers	4.9
Service workers	6.4
Non-farm laborers	12.4
Farmers and farm managers	0.3
Farm laborers and foremen	4.3

Source: *Manpower Report of the President and A Report on Manpower Resources, Utilization, and Training*, transmitted to the Congress March 1963 (Washington, D.C.: Government Printing Office, 1963), table A-8, p. 144, and tables A-9 and A-10, p. 145.

Table 4.70

MEDIAN EARNINGS[1] OF THE EXPERIENCED CIVILIAN LABOR FORCE, BY SEX, IN THE UNITED STATES, 1960

	Male	*Female*
Experienced civilian labor force	**$4,621**	**$2,257**
Professional, technical and kindred workers	6,619	3,625
Farm and farm managers	2,169	836
Managers, officials, and proprietors (excluding farm)	6,664	3,355
Clerical and kindred workers	4,785	3,017
Sales workers	4,987	1,498
Craftsmen, foremen and kindred workers	5,240	2,927
Operatives and kindred workers	4,299	2,319
Private household workers	1,078	684
Service workers (except private household)	3,310	1,385
Farm laborers and foremen	1,066	602
Laborers, except farm and mine	2,948	1,872

1. Earnings were obtained by summing wages or salary and self-employment income. It excludes income from such sources as social security, pensions, veteran's payments, rent, interest or dividends, unemployment insurance, welfare payments, etc. The figures shown here are the amounts received before deductions for taxes, social security, union dues, bond purchases, etc. (Source, p. xxxix.)

Source: *U. S. Census of Population: 1960*. Final Report PC(1)-1D, *op. cit.*, table 208, pp. 553-555.

Table 4.71

MEDIAN INCOME OF PERSONS WITH INCOME, BY SEX AND COLOR, IN THE UNITED STATES, 1949 AND 1959

	Both sexes	*Men*	*Women*
1949[1]			
White	$2,053	$2,573	$1,138
Non-white	973	1,361	590
Total	**1,918**	**2,434**	**1,029**
1959[2]			
White	$3,024	$4,319	$1,441
Non-white	1,502	2,273	909
Total	**2,798**	**4,103**	**1,357**

1. 1949 income data based on a 20% sample of the 1950 decennial census population 14 years old and over.
2. Based on a 25% sample of the 1960 decennial census population 14 years old and over.

Source: *U. S. Census of Population: 1960.* Final Report PC(1)–1C, *op. cit.*, table 97, pp. 228-229.

Table 4.72

THE CHANGING DISTRIBUTION OF INCOME IN THE UNITED STATES, 1929, 1947, AND 1960*

Family Incomes	*Per Cent with a Given Income*			*Share Each Income Group Had in Total Income*		
	1929	*1947*	*1960*	*1929*	*1947*	*1960*
Less than $4,000[1]	65.2	37.3	23.1	31.6	16.2	7.3
$4-6,000[2]	17.2	29.3	22.7	18.2	24.2	14.8
$6-7,500	6.1	12.4	16.2	8.7	13.9	14.2
$7,5-15,000	9.1	17.2	30.7	19.5	28.2	40.0
$15,000 or more	2.4	3.8	7.3	22.0	17.5	23.7
Unattached Individuals						
Less than $2,000[1]	49.0	46.8	36.6	20.8	18.7	11.8
$2-3,000[2]	22.0	22.6	19.7	21.7	21.8	15.2
$3-5,000	22.5	22.5	28.1	32.7	33.1	33.6
$5-$7,500	4.6	5.6	11.0	10.7	12.7	20.1
$7,500 or more	1.9	2.5	4.6	14.1	13.7	19.3

* All income data have been expressed as constant (1960) dollars.
1. Defined in source as poverty.
2. Defined in source as deprivation.

Source: Conference on Economic Progress, *Poverty and Deprivation in the U. S.: The Plight of Two-Fifths of a Nation* (Washington, D.C., 1962), pp. 26-27 and 37-38.

Table 4.80

Table 4.80

DISTRIBUTION OF CONSUMER EXPENDITURES AMONG VARIOUS CATEGORIES OF GOODS, SELECTED YEARS, 1929-1960

(Percentages based on current price totals)

	1929	*1939-41*	*1958-60*
Food and tobacco	26.9	31.1	27.3
Clothing	14.2	12.6	10.5
Personal care	1.4	1.4	1.6
Housing	14.5	12.8	12.8
House operation[1]	13.6	14.5	14.0
Medical and death expenses	4.5	4.8	6.3
Personal business	6.4	5.0	6.0
Transportation	9.6	9.9	12.1
Recreation	5.5	5.2	5.8
Education and research	0.8	0.9	1.3
Religion and domestic private welfare	1.5	1.4	1.4
Foreign travel and remittances	1.0	0.4	0.9
Total	**100.0**	**100.0**	**100.0**

1. Includes durable and non-durable household goods, utilities and fuel, and domestic services.

Source: Simon Kuznets, "Income Distribution and Changes in Consumption," in *The Changing American Population,* Hoke S. Simpson, ed. (New York: Institute of Life Insurance, 1962), table 8, pp. 46-47.

Table 4.81

PROPORTION OF ANNUAL EXPENDITURE ON VARIOUS CONSUMPTION ITEMS IN HOUSEHOLDS OF DIFFERENT INCOME IN THE UNITED STATES, 1955 - 1956[1]

	All households	*Annual Household Income* Under $2,000	$2,000-$2,999	$3,000-$3,999	$4,000-$4,999	$5,000-$6,999	$7,000-$9,999	$10,000 or more
All Goods and Services	**100%**	**100%**	**100%**	**100%**	**100%**	**100%**	**100%**	**100%**
Food, Beverages, and Tobacco	29	36	33	30	29	28	26	24
Clothing and Accessories	12	11	11	13	12	11	13	14
Medical and Personal Care	5	7	5	6	5	5	5	6
Home Operation and Improvement	19	17	20	18	19	19	18	18
Home Furnishings and Equipment	9	7	8	8	8	9	9	10
Recreation and Recreation Equipment	5	5	5	5	6	5	5	6
Automotive	14	11	13	15	14	16	15	15
Other Goods and Services	7	6	5	6	7	7	9	7

1. Panel study by A. Politz Research, Inc., of 10,243 households.

Source: *Life Study of Consumer Expenditure*, Time, Inc., New York, 1957, p. 20.

Table 4.82

NUMBER OF OCCUPIED DWELLING UNITS AND PER CENT DISTRIBUTION AMONG OWNERS AND TENANTS, BY RESIDENCE, IN THE UNITED STATES, FOR SELECTED DATES, 1900 - 1960

	Number (000,000's)	*Per Cent Owner-occupied*[2]	*Renter-occupied*
1900	16.0	46.7	53.3
1920	24.4	45.6	54.4
1940	34.9	43.6	56.4
1960	53.0	61.9	38.1
Non Farm			
1900	10.3	36.5	63.5
1960	49.5	61.0	39.0
Farm			
1900[1]	5.7	64.4	35.6
1960	3.6	73.8	26.2

1. Contains a small proportion of urban-farm families in addition to the rural-farm families.
2. Median value of owner-occupied nonfarm dwelling units (the amount estimated by owner-occupant that the property, including the structure and its land, would sell for under ordinary conditions and not at forced sale):
   1940 - $ 2,377
   1950 - $ 7,400
   1960 - $11,900

Source: *Statistical Abstract of the U. S. 1962, op. cit.*, table 1071, p. 758. (Median value from table 1076, p. 761.)
1940 median value from *Statistical Abstract of the U.S. 1959, op. cit.*, table 1039, p. 771.

Table 4.83

PERCENTAGE DISTRIBUTION OF CONSUMER EXPENDITURES FOR RECREATIONAL GOODS AND SERVICES, BY TYPE, 1909, 1934, AND 1959

	1909	*1934*	*1959*
Theatres and entertainment	19.4	26.8	10.0
Spectator sports	*	3.1	1.6
Clubs and fraternal organizations	14.1	9.5	4.6
Participant recreation	2.6	7.4	8.0
Reading	12.1	12.2	9.5
Gardening	8.1	5.6	5.6
Radios, TV's, and musical instruments	19.3	11.7	26.5
Sports equipment	16.6	15.2	26.9
Other	**	8.5	7.3

* Earliest date shown is 1921, for which date the percentage is 1.5.
** Earliest date: 1929; percentage then: 6.2.

Source: De Grazia, *op. cit.*, table 7, pp. 453-455.

Table 4.84
INTERNATIONAL COMPARISON OF MOTOR VEHICLES, RADIOS, TELEVISION, TELEPHONES, AND NEWSPAPERS IN SELECTED COUNTRIES, 1960

Ratio (number per 1,000 population)	*Motor Vehicles in Use*[1]	*Radio Receiving Sets*[2]	*Telephones in Use*[3]	*Newspaper Copies*[4]	*Television Receiving Sets*
United States	403	941	411	328[6]	297
United Kingdom	133	290	156	514	211
France	158	242	97	243[6]	42
Sweden	160	360	347	462[6]	133
Australia	262	223	214	380[5]	107
Brazil[7]	13[6]	65[6]	14	60[6]	17
India	1	5	1	11	*
Japan	19	157	59	397	64
U.S.S.R.	*	190[6]	*	172	24
World	**40**	**127**	**47**	*	**33**

* Not shown in source.
1. Footnotes in source indicate some minor sources of non-comparability.
2. Data based either on count of licenses issued or on estimates. In varying degrees, licensing fails to account for all sets.
3. Comprises public and private telephones (including extension instruments) connected to a central exchange.
4. No adjustment made for copies sold outside the country. The base (population) used for computing this ratio is for the same years as those shown in footnotes 5 and 6.
5. 1958.
6. 1959.
7. Source cited below shows an *estimated* total population for 1960 much lower than the *census* count obtained from the *Statistical Abstract of the U. S. 1962, op. cit.*, table 1243, p. 911.

Note: These data should be used with caution. The quality may vary considerably. See footnotes in the tables from which the data were obtained. Many further qualifications of the data have been omitted for lack of space.

Source: U.N. *Statistical Yearbook 1961* (New York, 1962), population: table 1, pp. 21ff. and table 1A, p. 41; newspapers, table 182, pp. 638-39; radios, table 185, pp. 646-647; cars, table 137, pp. 338-345; telephones, table 147, pp. 398-400; and TV, table 186, p. 648.

Table 4.85
PER CENT OF HOUSEHOLDS WITH TELEVISION SETS, BY RURAL-URBAN RESIDENCE, IN THE UNITED STATES, 1955, 1958, and 1961

Whole Country	*June 1955*	*Jan. 1958*	*May 1961*
No set	33	17	11
One set	65	76	77
Two sets or more	2	7	12
Per Cent with at least One Set			
Urban	74	87	90
Rural nonfarm	61	80	90
Rural farm	42	68	80

Source: *Statistical Abstract of the U. S. 1959, op. cit.*, table 668, p. 520, for 1958. For other two dates, *Statistical Abstract of the U.S. 1962, op. cit.*, table 705, p. 522.

Table 5.10

NUMBER OF NEW SCIENTIFIC BOOKS PUBLISHED IN THE UNITED STATES, BY SELECTED TYPE, FOR SELECTED YEARS, 1928 - 1962

	1928	*1938*	*1948*	*1958*	*1962*
Science (physical and natural)	340	423	412	781	1174
Technical[1]	246	319	344	443	780
Medicine[2]	240	293	235	393	688
Sociology and Economics	502	758	388	494	1603
History	394	776	432	750	812
Geography[3]	345	317	164	271	532
Total	**2,067**	**2,886**	**1,975**	**3,132**	**5,589**

1. From 1943 includes "military."
2. From 1933 includes "hygiene."
3. From 1933 includes "travel."

Source: *Publishers' Weekly,* R. R. Bowker Co., New York, generally the third issue in January of the year following the date shown.

Table 5.11

SCIENTIFIC BOOKS (INCLUDING RE-EDITIONS) PUBLISHED IN SELECTED COUNTRIES, 1960[1]

	USA[2]	*USSR*	*United Kingdom*[3]	*Sweden*
Pure science	1,089	5,061	1,879	538
Applied science	1,876	36,931	3,882	1,042
Social science	1,496	14,403	3,400	476
Geography and History	2,210	2,261	2,545	715
Philology	228	2,026	734	426
Philosophy	480	612	457	45
Total	**7,379**	**61,294**	**12,897**	**3,242**

1. "The data show by subjects the number of books published, each title being counted as one unit; they are understood, unless otherwise stated, to cover all non-periodical publications, including pamphlets, first editions of originals and (new) translations, re-editions and the more important government reports." (Source, p. 633.)
2. "Books only, excluding pamphlets which are defined as works of less than 49 pages. The statistics refer only to the production of the book trade (namely, the industry engaged in the publishing of books for sale to the general public) and omit a large part of total book production (publications of the federal, state and local governments, universities, churches, and other organizations, most reports and accounts of proceedings, dissertations, laboratory manuals, wordbooks)." (Source, p. 633.)
3. "Including books published in Ireland. Books and pamphlets priced at less than sixpence are omitted." (Source, p. 633)

Source: United Nations, *Statistical Yearbook 1961,* New York, 1961, table 179, pp. 630-633.

Table 5.20

FUNDS FOR RESEARCH AND DEVELOPMENT AND FOR BASIC RESEARCH, 1953-54 AND 1960-61[1]

(in millions of dollars)

	Research and Development[2] 1953-54	*Research and Development*[2] 1960-61 (prel.)	*Basic Research* 1953-54	*Basic Research* 1960-61 (prel.)
Sources of Funds				
Federal government[3]	2,740	9,220	195	745
Industry	2,240	4,490	147	313
Colleges and universities[4]	130	210	62	161
Other non-profit institutions[4]	40	120	28	83
Use of funds by				
Federal government	970	2,060	47	245
Industry[5]	3,630	10,500	151	382
Colleges and universities[5]	450	1,200	208	575
Other non-profit institutions[5]	100	280	26	100
Total	**5,150**	**14,040**	**432**	**1,302**

1. Includes Alaska and Hawaii, except industry data for 1953-54. "Data refer in general to the natural sciences; however, some funds for psychology and the social sciences could not be eliminated."
2. "Includes basic research, applied research and development."
3. Data based on reports from those who performed the research.
4. "Includes State and local funds received by these institutions and used for research and development."
5. "Includes expenditures at Federal contract research centers administered by organizations in this sector."

Note: These data and those published in the previous edition of the *Almanac* are not comparable. The original source of these data is the National Science Foundation; of the previous data, the Department of Defense. For reasons not explained in the *Statistical Abstract,* there are substantial differences at some points between these two sets of data.

Source: U. S. Bureau of the Census, *Statistical Abstract of the U.S.: 1962* (Washington, D.C., 1962), table 734 p. 542.

Table 5.30

NUMBER OF SCHOOLS OF SPECIFIED TYPE, AND NUMBER OF TEACHERS AND PUPILS IN EACH TYPE IN THE UNITED STATES, 1958

Type of School	*Schools*	*Pupils (000's)*	*Instructional Staff (000's)*
Public			
Elementary	98,310[1]	24,014[2]	1,340 (Elementary and Secondary)
Secondary	25,606	7,895	
Higher	668	1,877	*
Non-public			
Elementary	13,170	4,297	164.6 (Elementary and Secondary)
Secondary	4,026	931	
Higher	1,266	1,407	*

* Public and non-public combined total 344,525.
1. Excludes kindergarten.
2. Excludes kindergarten, which totalled 1,786,000.

Source: *Statistical Abstract of the U. S. 1962, op. cit.*, schools: table 138, p. 111; pupils: table 155, p. 122 and table 139, p. 111; and teachers: table 154, p. 121, table 164, p. 128, and table 170, p. 132.

Table 5.31

AVERAGE LENGTH OF THE SCHOOL TERM IN THE UNITED STATES, 1900, 1940 AND 1960

	1900	*1940*	*1960*
Average length of term (in days)	144.3	175.0	178.0
Average number of days attended (per enrolled student)	99.0	151.7	160.2

Source: *Statistical Abstract of the U. S. 1962, op. cit.*, table 154, p. 121.

Table 5.40

ILLITERACY[1] IN THE UNITED STATES, 1900-1960[2]

Year	*Per cent*
1900	11.3
1910	8.3
1920	6.5
1930	4.8
1940	*
1950	3.3
1960	2.4

* Not shown in the source.

1. "Illiteracy" is defined as the inability to read and write a simple message either in English or in any language. It should be distinguished from "functional illiteracy," which refers to persons who have completed less than five years of school. In 1960 there were about three million illiterates but about eight million functional illiterates.

2. Data refer to population age 15 or more from 1900 to 1930, and to population age 14 or more in 1950 and 1960.

Source: U. S. Bureau of the Census, *Current Population Reports,* Series P-23, No. 8 (Feb. 12, 1963), pp. 1-2.

Table 5.41

PERCENTAGE OF FIFTH-GRADERS GRADUATING FROM HIGH SCHOOL AND ENTERING COLLEGE, SELECTED DATES, 1931 - 1960

Year of Entrance into Fifth Grade	*Graduated from H.S.*[1] *Year*	*% of 5th Graders*	*First-time Coll. Students % of 5th Gr.*	*Ratio: Coll. Beginners to H.S. Grads.*
1923	1931	27.0	12.2	.45
1928	1936	37.8	13.7	.36
1933	1941	46.2	14.2	.31
1938	1946	41.9	*	—
1943	1951	52.4	21.8	.42
1948	1956	58.1	30.1	.53
1952 (preliminary)	1960	60.4	31.9	.53

* Estimate not reliable.

1. As per cent of persons 17 years old, the data for high school graduates since 1920 are:

	Number of graduates (000's)	*Per cent*
1920	311	16.8
1930	667	29.0
1940	1,221	50.8
1950	1,200	59.8
1958	1,506	64.8

Source: U. S. Department of Health, Education and Welfare, *Health, Education and Welfare Trends, 1961 Edition* (Washington, D.C.: Government Printing Office, 1961), p. 40.

Table 5.42

PROJECTIONS TO 1970 OF SCHOOL AND COLLEGE ENROLLMENT[1] (in millions)

	Estimated 1955	*Estimated 1960*	*Projected 1965*	*Projected 1970*
All school levels	37.4	46.3	52.5	57.3
Elementary school and kindergarten	27.1	32.4	35.4	37.9
High school	8.0	10.3	12.7	14.1
College and professional school	2.4	3.6	4.4	5.3

1. Source shows eleven projections, carried beyond 1970. The projection shown here is based on the assumptions that the fertility levels experienced in the 1955-57 period will continue to 1970 and that the enrollment percentage will remain constant at the 1957-59 average annual level.

Source: U. S. Bureau of the Census, *Current Population Reports, Population Estimates,* Series P-25, no. 232 (June 22, 1961), table B, p. 2.

Table 5.50

PER CENT OF THE POPULATION 5-24 YEARS OF AGE ENROLLED IN SCHOOL, BY AGE, IN THE UNITED STATES, 1920, 1940 AND 1960

Age	*Per Cent* 1920	1940	1960[1]
5 and 6 years	41.0	43.0	63.7
7-13 years	90.6	95.0	97.5
14 and 15 years	79.9	90.0	94.1
16 and 17 years	42.9	68.7	80.9
18 and 19 years	17.8	28.9	42.4
20-24 years	*	6.6	14.6

* Not available.

1 Excludes Alaska and Hawaii.

Source: *U. S. Census of Population: 1960*. Final Report PC(1)-1C, *op. cit.*, table 74, p. 206.

Table 5.51

PER CENT OF PERSONS AGED 16 - 24 WITH SOME COLLEGE ATTENDANCE (INCLUDING THOSE CURRENTLY ENROLLED), BY FAMILY INCOME, AND EDUCATIONAL STATUS OF FATHER, OCTOBER 1960

		Educational Status of Father		
Family income	*All Persons Aged 16-24*	*Did not Graduate from High School*	*Graduated from High Sch. but did not Attend Coll.*	*Attended College but did not Graduate*
Less than $5,000	19.0	12.6	41.5	52.3
$5,000 - 7,500	33.0	23.1	44.4	73.4
$7,500 - $10,000	48.6	32.9	57.7	82.9
$10,000 or more	60.3	40.8	50.0	88.6

Source: U. S. Bureau of the Census, *Current Population Reports, Population Characteristics,* Series P-20, no. 110 (July 24, 1961), table 10, p. 15.

Table 5.52

PER CENT OF PERSONS AGED 16-24 CURRENTLY ENROLLED IN COLLEGE, BY COLOR AND SEX, BY EDUCATIONAL STATUS OF FATHER, OCTOBER 1960*

White and Nonwhite	*All Persons Aged 16-24*	*Educational Status of Father*			
		Not High School Graduate	*H.S. Grad. But no Coll. Attendance*	*Some College*	*Graduated from College*
Both sexes	18.0	10.6	25.0	42.8	56.4
Male	24.6	14.7	35.9	51.9	71.3
Female	12.5	7.1	15.7	35.0	43.0
Nonwhite only					
Both sexes	9.3	7.0	18.3	–	–
Male	10.7	7.2	–	–	–
Female	8.1	6.8	–	–	–

* Percent not shown where base is less than 150,000.

Source: *ibid.*, table 9, p. 15.

Table 5.53

EDUCATIONAL ATTAINMENT OF MEN AGED 20-24, BY EDUCATIONAL STATUS OF FATHER, OCTOBER 1960

(Per cent distribution)

Educational Attainment	*All Men Aged 20-42*	*Educational Status of Father*			
		Not High School Graduate	*H.S. Grad. But no Coll. Att.*	*Some College*	*Graduated from College*
	100.0	**100.0**	**100.0**	**100.0**	**100.0**
No high school diploma	32.2	42.6	10.3	6.5	4.0
High school diploma but no college attendance	32.4	34.1	36.1	23.8	8.2
Some college	10.2	7.8	17.4	15.8	10.1
Currently enrolled In college	19.5	12.0	28.2	40.4	61.9
College graduate	5.7	3.5	8.1	13.5	15.9

Source: *ibid.*, table A, p. 1.

Table 5.54

MEDIAN YEARS OF SCHOOL COMPLETED BY PERSONS 25 YEARS OLD AND OVER, BY COLOR, IN THE UNITED STATES, 1940, 1950, AND 1960

	1940[1]	*1950*	*1960*
White	8.7	9.7	10.9
Non-White	5.7	6.9	8.2
All	**8.6**	**9.3**	**10.6**

1. 1940 was the first decennial census in which data concerning educational attainment were gathered.

Sources: 1) 1940–U. S. Bureau of the Census, *U. S. Census of Population: 1940,* Vol. 4, *Characteristics by Age,* Part 1, U. S. Summary, U. S. Government Printing Office, Washington, D. C., 1943, table 23, p. 89.
2) 1950–*U.S. Census of Population: 1950,* Vol. 2, *op. cit.,* table 44, p. 96.
3) 1960–*U. S. Census of Population: 1960.* Final Report PC(1)-1C, *op. cit.,* table 76, p. 207.

Table 5.55

MEDIAN YEARS OF SCHOOL COMPLETED BY PERSONS 25 YEARS OLD AND OVER, BY AGE, SEX, AND COLOR, IN THE UNITED STATES, 1960

	Males		*Females*	
	White	*Nonwhite*	*White*	*Nonwhite*
25-29	12.4	10.5	12.3	11.1
30-34	12.2	9.7	12.3	10.5
35-39	12.2	8.9	12.2	9.7
40-44	12.0	8.3	12.1	8.7
45-49	10.7	7.4	11.2	8.1
50-54	9.8	6.8	10.4	7.6
55-59	8.8	6.0	9.2	6.9
60-64	8.6	5.5	8.8	6.4
65-69	8.4	4.7	8.6	5.6
70-74	8.2	4.4	8.5	5.2
75 years and over	8.1	3.9	8.4	4.5
25 years and over	**10.6**	**7.9**	**11.0**	**8.5**

Source: *U. S. Census of Population: 1960.* Final Report PC(1)-1D, *op. cit.,* table 173, pp. 406-407.

Table 5.60
INCOME OF MEN AGED 25 AND OLDER WITH VARIOUS LEVELS OF EDUCATION IN THE UNITED STATES, 1958

Years of school completed	*Mean income for the year*[1]	*Lifetime income*[2]
Elementary		
Less than 8	$2,551	$120,965
8	3,769	169,976
High school		
1-3	4,618	198,881
4	5,567	241,844
College		
1-3	6,966	305,395
4 years or more	9,206	419,871

1. Total money income, derived from the consumer income supplements to the March, 1959 *Current Population Survey* of the U. S. Census Bureau.
2. Total money income, derived by:
   a) estimating the number of survivors to working age among a hypothetical cohort of 100,000;
   b) of these, estimating the number of man-years these survivors would live until the last one died;
   c) assuming that during each year of life, these men would receive an average income corresponding to that received by men in the same age group with the same amount of education.

   For more information, see the source.

Source: Herman P. Miller, "Annual and Lifetime Income in Relation to Education: 1939-1959," *The American Economic Review,* vol. L, No. 5 (Dec., 1960), table 1, p. 966 and table 11, p. 981.

Table 5.61
MEDIAN YEARS OF SCHOOL COMPLETED BY EMPLOYED MALES 18 YEARS OLD AND OVER, BY OCCUPATION GROUP, IN THE UNITED STATES, MARCH 1959[1]

Occupation Group	*Median*
Professional, technical and kindred workers	16.4
Medical and other health workers	17+
Teachers, except college	17+
Other professional, technical, and kindred workers	16.1
Managers, officials, and proprietors (except farm)	12.4
Salaried workers	12.7
Self-employed workers	12.0
Clerical and kindred workers	12.5
Sales workers	12.6
Craftsmen, foremen, and kindred workers	11.0
Operatives and kindred workers	10.0
Service workers	10.1
Farmers and farm managers	8.7
Farm laborers and foremen	7.7
Laborers, except farm and mine	8.5

1. Civilian "noninstitutional" population.

Source: U. S. Bureau of the Census, *Current Population Reports,* Series P-20, No. 99, table E, p. 5.

Table 6.10

COMPARISON OF RELIGIOUS ACTIVITY IN GREAT BRITAIN AND THE UNITED STATES, 1940's AND 1950's[1]

	Per Cent of Total Population	
	Great Britain	*U.S.A.*
Church members	22	57
Weekly attendance (reported)	15	43
Daily prayer (reported)	46	43
Believe in God	72	96
Believe in After-life	47	72
Could name four gospels	61	35
Claim affiliation	91	95

1. Based on sample surveys of varying quality.

Source: Michael Argyle, *Religious Rehavior*, The Free Press, Glencoe, Ill., table 8, p. 35.

Table 6.20

RELIGION REPORTED BY THE CIVILIAN POPULATION 14 YEARS OLD AND OVER, BY SEX AND BY RESIDENCE, IN THE UNITED STATES, MARCH 1957[1]

	Number (000's)	*Per Cent of Total*	*Per Cent that is Female*	*Per Cent that is Urban*
Protestant	78,952	66.2	52.9	56.7
Baptist	23,525	19.7	52.5	*
Lutheran	8,417	7.1	51.3	*
Methodist	16,676	14.0	53.5	*
Presbyterian	6,656	5.6	54.1	*
Other Protestant	23,678	19.8	53.2	*
Roman Catholic	30,669	25.7	51.9	78.8
Jewish	3,868	3.2	51.9	96.1
Other religion	1,545	1.3	49.8	77.4
No religion	3,195	2.7	26.2	54.2
Religion not reported	1,104	0.9	50.4	68.2
Total	**119,333**	**100.0**	**51.8**	**63.9**

* Not available.

1. These data were obtained in the usual Census Bureau monthly nation-wide sample survey of the population 14 years old or more. The question, "What is your religion?" was answered on a voluntary basis. The question did not relate to church membership, attendance at church services or gatherings, or religious beliefs.

"For various reasons, the present data on religion are not comparable with the membership reports issued by such organizations themselves. The number of persons in the various religious groups shown here tend to exceed the number of members of comparable age shown in the membership reports. This report is limited to persons 14 years old and over, although some religious organizations report infants and young children as members. The present data count each person once and only once, whereas in the membership reports of the organizations a person may be counted as a member by more than one group or he may not be counted as a member of any group. The wide differences between the figures for some groups in the present report and in reports obtained from the religious organizations reflect the fact that the present data are not limited to persons who hold formal membership in any group. In addition, the survey figures are subject to sampling error and some error of response . . ., and the records of organizations vary in the degree to which they are complete and up-to-date."

(from *Current Population Reports*, Series P-20, Number 79, pp. 1 and 3.)

Source: *Statistical Abstract of the U. S. 1958, op. cit.*, table 52, p. 50.

Table 6.30

SOCIAL AND ECONOMIC CHARACTERISTICS OF MAJOR RELIGIOUS GROUPS IN THE UNITED STATES, 1957-58[1]

		Sex	*Marital Status*	*Fertility*		*Education*	*Occupation*	*Church Attendance*
Religious Groups	*Sample Size*[2]	*Per Cent Women*	*Per Cent Married*	*Per Cent Childless*	*Per Cent with Three or More Children*	*Per Cent with Some College*	*Per cent who are either in Professions or are Owners, Mgrs., or Officials*	*Per Cent Attending at least once a month*
Nation	**5,827**	**54**	**82**	**44**	**22**	**19**	**21**	**66**
Protestants	4,185	55	82	43	22	19	21	62
Baptists	939	58	80	42	25	11	13	72
White	713	56	83	41	25	11	17	*
Negro	226	66	68	41	29	6	5	*
Methodists	730	56	81	46	21	21	21	63
Lutherans	328	54	81	43	24	14	18	68
Presbyterians	272	58	78	48	16	36	33	61
Episcopalians	119	65	79	53	15	53	46	56
Roman Catholics	1,270	54	82	39	27	14	19	85
Jews	188	58	85	40	16	33	51	34
No religion	125	19	77	48	23	22	25	3

* Not shown in source.

1. These data were obtained from three national sample surveys carried out by the Survey Research Center of The University of Michigan. Two of the three were done in the spring of 1957, and third in November, 1958. The author of the source article asserts that "the passage of 18 months [between spring, 1957 and November, 1958] produced only random changes." (footnote 3, p. 569.)
2. Measures of sampling error are provided in the source article. Readers desiring more reliable estimates than the data shown here are urged to consult the source. As some indication of the sizes of the errors, it may be noted that for Protestants as a whole, two standard errors (corresponding to the .05 level of confidence) range from 1.8 per cent to 2.2 per cent, depending on the size of the estimated percentage. At the other extreme, two standard errors for the Episcopalians range from about 9.5 per cent to about 13.5 per cent.

Source: Bernard Lazerwitz, "A Comparison of Major U. S. Religious Groups," *Journal of the American Statistical Association*, vol. 56, no. 295 (September, 1961), pp. 568-579.

Table 7.10

ARTISTIC OCCUPATIONS IN THE UNITED STATES, 1950 AND 1960

	1950 Experienced Civilian Labor Force		*1960 Experienced Civilian Labor Force*	
	(000's)	*Per cent*	*(000's)*	*Per cent*
Actors	18.3	0.03	13.5	0.02
Architects	23.9	0.04	30.5	0.04
Artists and Art Teachers	80.8	0.14	104.7	0.15
Authors	16.2	0.03	28.7	0.04
Dancers and Dancing Teachers	17.4	0.03	21.9	0.03
Entertainers (not elsewhere classified	16.4	0.03	12.2	0.02
Musicians and Music Teachers	162.0	0.27	197.5	0.29
Photographers	55.0	0.09	53.1	0.08
Total Artistic Occupations	390.0	0.66	462.1	0.67
All Professional, Technical and Kindred Workers	5,000.5	8.4	7,335.7	10.8
Total Experienced Civilian Labor Force	59,229.5	100.0	67,990.1	100.0

Source: U. S. Bureau of the Census. *U. S. Census of Population: 1960. Detailed Characteristics. United States Summary.* Final Report PC(1)-1D (Washington, D.C.: Government Printing Office, 1963), table 201, p. 522.

Table 7.20
INCOME OF YOUNG PAINTERS

Average Annual Income from Art 1950-1954[2]	*Number of Respondents in*	
	Mail Survey	*Personal Interviews*
Nothing	20	8
Under $200	27	12
$200 - 499	24	5
$500 - 999	17	8
$1,000 - 1,999	10	5
$2,000 - 2,999	7	6
$3,000 and over	8	3
No reply	21	3
Supplement to Artistic Income (Multiple answers)		
Self-employment	82	29
Spouse's employment	14	12
Annuities, trust fund, etc.	13	4
Other	5	5
None	2	1
No reply	24	1

1. Due to difficulties in defining a population of "artists" in the New York metropolitan area, the sample was restricted to "a group of artists who within the preceding three years had exhibited or been classified for exhibition with recognized art organizations," the Audubon Society of Artists, the Whitney Museum of American Art, the New York City Art Center Gallery, the National Academy of Design and the Museum of Modern Art. From lists supplied by these organizations a random sample of 300 cases was drawn. From this sample a sub-sample of 50 cases was drawn for interviewing. The remaining 250 received a mail questionnaire. A total of 134 (54%) replied to this questionnaire. None of the 50 respondents refused to be interviewed. The study was conducted by Dr. Bernard S. Myers for the New York Area Research Council of The City College of New York.

2. In an earlier mail survey of 500 artists, of which 200 replied, "the average gross income of the 'leading' artists, from all sources, was $4,144 in 1944-45, while for the ten-year period preceding that date the average had been $2,808 per year . . ." However, average income from art sales *alone* was only $1,154. The range was $50 to $8,500. (Source, pp. 1-2.)

Source: Bernard S. Myers, *Problems of the Younger American Artist*, The City College Press, New York, 1957, table V, Section D.b. and E, pp. 62-63.

Table 7.30

PER CENT OF U.S. POPULATION ENGAGING IN VARIOUS LEISURE ACTIVITIES "YESTERDAY,"[1] BY PERSONAL CHARACTERISTICS, 1957[2]

Activity	*Per Cent of all Respondents*	*Age*[3]			*Sex*		*Education of those 20 or more years old*[4]			*Annual Family Income*[5]	
		15-19	*50-59*	*60 and over*	*Men*	*Women*	*Less than 8th grade*	*8th grade*	*College*	*Under $3,000*	*$7,000 and over*
Watching television	57	56	56	53	56	57	51	56	55	47	59
Visiting friends, relatives	38	46	33	37	32	42	38	35	36	39	39
Working in yard, garden	33	20	38	42	36	34	35	36	37	35	34
Reading magazines	27	31	23	27	25	27	12	19	40	23	33
Reading books	18	21	15	21	17	18	12	15	30	20	20
Going pleasure driving	17	25	11	11	15	16	10	11	18	13	17
Listening to records	14	35	6	6	9	13	8	8	13	13	15
Going to meetings or other organization activities	11	11	11	12	10	11	11	8	14	11	11
Special hobbies	10	11	12	11	8	12	9	9	11	8	11
Going out to dinner	8	7	8	6	7	9	5	6	12	6	12
Participating in sports	8	26	3	2	8	4	3	4	9	3	11
Playing cards, checkers, etc.	7	12	5	6	6	7	5	7	7	5	8
None of those listed	7	3	8	9	8	8	13	9	5	10	6

All footnotes on p. 88.

Table 7.30 (Continued)

Activity	Per Cent of all Respondents	Age[3] 15-19	50-59	60 and over	Sex Men	Women	Education of those 20 or more years old[4] Less than 8th grade	8th grade	College	Annual Family Income[5] Under $3,000	$7,000 and over
Spending time at drug store, etc.	6	20	3	1	5	3	3	3	4	5	7
Singing or playing musical instrument	5	10	3	3	4	4	3	3	7	5	4
Going to see sports events	4	7	4	2	5	2	1	3	4	3	5
Going to movies in theatre	3	9	2	1	2	3	3	2	3	3	4
Going to drive-in movies	2	6	1	0	2	2	1	1	1	1	2
Going to dances	2	8	1	0	1	1	2	1	2	2	1
Going to a play, concert, or opera	1	1	0	1	0	1	1	1	1	1	1
Going to lectures or adult school	1	1	1	1	1	1	1	0	1	0	1

1. Day before the one on which the respondent was interviewed.
2. Data based on personal interviews with a national probability sample of 5,021 persons, representing the total U. S. population, 15 years old or more, living in private households. More detail about sample given in the source, page 463.
3. The source shows also the three age classes, 20-29, 30-39, and 40-49. With only five exceptions, none of the percentages in these classes differed from those shown for all respondents by more than three percentage points. The exceptions were: age 20-29, 24% "working around the yard and in garden," and 21% "going pleasure driving"; age 40-49, 61% "watching television,"; 39% "reading magazines," and 10% listening to records."
4. The source shows also the two education categories "high school (incomplete)" and "high school (complete)." With only one exception none of the percentages in these categories differed from those shown for all respondents by more than three percentage points. The one exception was: 61% of those who completed high schcool were "watching television."
5. The source shows also the two income categories $3,000-$4,999 and $5,000-$6,999. None of the percentages in these two categories, without exception, differed from those shown for all respondents by more than three percentage points.

Source: Sebastian De Grazia, *Of Time, Work and Leisure* (New York: Twentieth Century Fund, 1962), table 8, pp. 460-463.

Table 8.10

VARIATIONS IN "TOLERANCE OF POLITICAL AND RELIGIOUS DEVIANTS" WITH RESPECT TO EDUCATION, OCCUPATION AND COMMUNITY POWER IN THE UNITED STATES, 1954

	Proportion Who Are "More Tolerant"[1]	*Number of Cases*
Education		
College Graduates	66%	(308)
Some College	53	(319)
High School Graduates	42	(768)
Some High School	29	(576)
Grade School	16	(792)
Occupation (Men only)		
Professional and Semi-Professional	66%	(159)
Proprietors, Managers and Officials	51	(223)
Clerical and Sales	49	(200)
Manual Workers[2]	30	(685)
Farmers or Farm Workers[2]	20	(202)
Power		
Community Leaders	66%	(1500)
Population in same cities as leaders	32	(897)
Nation, rural and urban	31	(4933)

1. According to a scale based on 15 questions dealing with willingness to tolerate non-conformists who are admitted or alleged Communists, advocates of government ownership of industry, and atheists. (See Appendix C in source.)
2. Computed by Professor S. M. Lipset for his book, *Political Man*, Doubleday and Co., New York, 1959, Table II, p. 104.

Source: Samuel A. Stouffer, *Communism, Conformity and Civil Liberties*, Doubleday and Co., New York, 1955, pp. 51, 90 and 139.

Table 8.20

READINESS TO DESEGREGATE IN A SOUTHERN COUNTY

Score	*Education* Mean No. Yrs. Completed	*Education* Per Cent With At Least 9 Yrs.	*Occupation* Per Cent White Collar	*Occupation* Per Cent Professional	*Income* Mean Annual	*Exposure to Mass-Media* Index
0*	10.1	72.0	71.4	22.4	$6,194	2.84
1	9.7	67.8	64.4	10.2	5,915	2.52
2	9.3	62.3	64.2	9.4	4,940	2.69
3	9.5	64.8	58.6	5.7	4,592	2.32
4**	8.0	40.7	35.8	1.8	3,500	2.06

* High readiness to accept desegregation. The higher the score the greater the resistance to desegregation.

** The highest score was given to those who were ready to use force to prevent desegregation.

Note: This information has been obtained from 287 white males, 18 years of age or older, in the labor force in Guilford County, North Carolina.

Source: Melvin M. Tumin, *Desegregation* (Princeton: Princeton University Press, 1958), table 56, p. 177.

Table 8.30

DEGREE OF COLOR SEGREGATION IN SCHOOLS IN SOUTHERN AND BORDER STATES, 1963-64

	Number of Negroes Enrolled in Public Grade Schools (000's)	*Per Cent of Negroes in Schools with Whites*
Alabama	287.4	0.004
Mississippi	292.0	---
South Carolina	259.0	0.004
Georgia	337.5	0.052
Louisiana	301.4	0.602
North Carolina	346.7	0.538
Arkansas	112.0	0.968
Virginia	236.4	1.57
Florida	237.9	1.53
Tennessee	164.9	2.71
Texas	326.4	4.29
Oklahoma	42.9	28.1
Missouri	95.0	42.1
Maryland	160.9	48.3
Kentucky[1]	54.9	54.4
Delaware	18.4	55.4
West Virginia	21.0*	87.9
District of Columbia	117.9	83.8

Source: *Statistical Summary of School Segregation-Desegregation in Southern and Border States, 1963-64,* The Southern Educational Reporting Service, Nashville, Tenn., 1963, p. 2.

* Figure corrected from source in personal communication.

[1] 1962-63.

Table 9.10

PER CENT OF WORLD'S POPULATION LIVING IN CITIES, BY SIZE OF CITY, FOR SELECTED DATES, 1800 - 1950

Year	*Per Cent* Cities of 20,000 or more	Cities of 100,000 or more
1800	2.4	1.7
1850	4.3	2.3
1900	9.2	5.5
1950	20.9	13.1

Source: Kingsley Davis, "The Origin and Growth of Urbanization in the World," *American Journal of Sociology*, Vol. 60 (1955), table 1, p. 433.

Table 9.11

PER CENT OF WORLD'S POPULATION LIVING IN CITIES, BY REGIONS, BY SIZE OF CITY, 1950

	Per Cent Cities of 20,000 or more	Cities of 100,000 or more
World	**21**	**13**
Oceania	47	41
North America[1]	42	29
Europe[2]	35	21
U.S.S.R.	31	18
South America	26	18
Middle America[3]	21	12
Asia[2]	13	8
Africa	9	5

1. Includes United States and Canada.
2. Without U.S.S.R.
3. Includes countries of Central America and the islands of the Caribbean.

Source: Kingsley Davis and Hilda Hertz, "The World Distribution of Urbanization," *Bulletin of the International Statistical Institute*, Vol. XXXIII (1953), Part IV, 3, p. 230.

Table 9.12

PER CENT OF THE TOTAL POPULATION LIVING IN URBAN AND RURAL AREAS, BY REGIONS, IN THE UNITED STATES, SELECTED DATES, 1850-1960

	U.S.	*Northeast*	*North Central*	*South*	*West*
1850:					
Urban	**15.3**	26.5	9.2	8.3	6.4
Rural	**84.7**	73.5	90.8	91.7	93.6
1900:					
Urban	**39.7**	66.1	38.6	18.0	40.6
Rural	**60.3**	33.9	61.4	82.0	59.4
1950:					
Urban[1]	**64.0**	79.5	64.1	48.6	69.8
Rural[1]	**36.0**	20.5	35.9	51.4	30.2
1960:					
Urban[2]	**69.9**	80.2	68.8	58.5	77.5
Rural[2]	**30.1**	19.8	31.2	41.5	22.5

1. A new urban definition was adopted for the 1950 census. The new definition more adequately includes large and densely settled places, even though they are not incorporated places. For the precise definition and a discussion of the differences between the new definition and the old one, see *U. S. Census of Population: 1950,* Vol. 2, *op. cit.,* pp. 9 and 11.
2. Substantially the same definition as the one used for the 1950 census.

Source: Taeuber and Taeuber, *op. cit.,* table 37, p. 122, for all dates except 1960. For 1960, *U. S. Census of Population: 1960.* Final Report PC(1)-1B, *op. cit.,* table 58, p. 166.

Table 9.13

PER CENT OF THE TOTAL POPULATION LIVING IN URBAN PLACES, BY RACE AND NATIVITY, IN THE UNITED STATES, 1900 AND 1960

	1900		*1960*[1]	
White	42.4		69.5	
Native		38.1		68.4
Foreign born		66.0		87.1
Negro	22.7		73.4	
Other races	20.8		58.3	
All	**40.0**		**69.8**	

1. Per Cent Increase, 1950-1960:

	Total	*White*	*Non-White*
Urban	29.3	27.1	48.7
Urbanized areas	38.4	35.3	64.9
Central cities	19.8	13.3	63.3
Urban fringe	81.5	81.8	75.0
Otherd urban	6.6	6.9	3.9
Rural	— 0.8	0.2	— 8.8

(*U.S. Census of Population : 1960.* Final Report PC(1)-1B, *op. cit.,* table 42, p. 143.)

Source: For 1900, Taeuber and Taeuber, *op. cit.,* table 38, p. 124.
For 1960, U. S. Bureau of the Census, *U. S. Census of Population: 1960. Detailed Characteristics. United States Summary.* Final Report PC(1)-1D. (Washington, D.C.: Government Printing Office, 1963), table 158, p. 359.

Table 9.14

GROWTH OF STANDARD METROPOLITAN STATISTICAL AREAS IN THE UNITED STATES, 1900, 1950, AND 1960[1]

	1900		*1950*		*1960*	
U. S. Population	76 million		151 Million		179 million	
SMSA[1] Population: Persons	31 million		86 million		113 million	
SMSA Population: Per Cent of U.S.	41%		57%		63%	
Distribution of SMSA Population:						
Central Cities	61.9%		57.7%		51.4%	
Other:	38.1		42.3		48.6	
Urban		13.5		21.2		36.8
Rural		24.6		21.1		11.8
Total SMSA Population	**100.0**		**100.0**		**100.0**	

1. The "standard metropolitan area" (SMA) was first defined for the 1950 census. In 1960 the title was changed to Standard Metropolitan Statistical Area (SMSA). The definition "associates with a central city of 50,000 or more the county (or counties) in which it is located and the adjoining county or counties which meet certain prescribed conditions of integration with the central city." (Source No. 1, p. 127. For the precise definition, see census publications.) In order to compare 1900 with 1950 or 1960, one could use for both dates either *only* those places which already had a central city of 50,000 or more in 1900, or *all* places which had (at least) one central city of 50,000 or more in 1950 or 1960, whether or not they had one such large city in 1900. The latter group of SMA's has been used to make the comparison shown in this table. There were 162 of them in 1950 and 212 in 1960. This exaggerates the siz of the population that lived in 1900 in areas that meet the criteria of the SMA definition. Actually, there were 24 million in such areas, which is less than 32% of the total U. S. population at that date.

Source: 1) For 1900 and 1950, Taeuber and Taeuber, *op. cit.*, table 41, p. 132, and table 45, p. 140.
2) For 1960, *U. S. Census of Population: 1960*. Final Report PC(1)-1C, *op. cit.*, table 101, p. 237.

Table 9.20

NUMBER OF COMMERCIAL BROADCASTING STATIONS ON THE AIR IN THE UNITED STATES FOR SELECTED DATES, 1945 - 1960[1]

	Total	*AM Radio*	*FM Radio*	*Television*
1945	936	884	46	6
1950	2,881	2,051	733	97
1955	3,627	2,635	553	439
1960	4,611	3,416	678	517[2]

1. As of Jan. 1. Includes Alaska, Hawaii, Puerto Rico, Virgin Islands, and, beginning in 1956, Guam.
2. Comparing the data for "television" in the 1962 *Statistical Abstract* with the data in the 1959 edition, from which the same kind of data was taken and published in the previous edition of the *Almanac*, shows an apparent downward revision, beginning with the figures for 1953.

Source: *Statistical Abstract of the U. S. 1962, op. cit.*, table 700, p. 520.

Table 9.21

NUMBER AND CIRCULATION OF NEWSPAPERS AND PERIODICALS IN THE UNITED STATES, FOR SELECTED DATES, 1929 - 1958

	Newspapers[1]		*Periodicals*	
	Number	*Aggregate Circulation (000's)*	*Number*	*Aggregate Circulation (000's)*
1929	10,176	91,778	5,157	202,022
1939	9,173	96,476	4,985	239,693
1947	10,282	119,567	4,610	384,628
1954	9,022	136,353	3,427	449,285
1958[2]	8,645	136,803	4,455	391,936

1. Newspaper circulation per family:

	Daily	*Sunday*
1940	1.17	0.92
1945	1.28	1.06
1950	1.23	1.06
1955	1.16	0.97
1958	1.14	0.93
1960	1.12	0.91

2. Not comparable with 1954 (and, presumably, earlier) data in a number of respects. For newspapers, "no separate data were collected in 1958 for newspapers published tri-weekly, semi-weekly, 'other.' Comparable totals for 1954 would be:

Total number of newspapers	8,589
Aggregate circulation	133,096,000."

For periodicals, "excludes any estimated circulation of the relatively small number of publications for which the circulation was not reported." (See source 2.)

Source: For 1929, *Statistical Abstract of the U. S. 1959, op. cit.*, table 669, p. 521. For other dates, *Statistical Abstract of the U. S. 1962, op. cit., tables* 706 and 707, p. 523.